an introduction to:
THE ART OF THEATRE

A comprehensive text — past, present, and future

TEACHER'S GUIDE

MARSH CASSADY

MERIWETHER PUBLISHING LTD.
Colorado Springs, Colorado

Meriwether Publishing Ltd., Publisher
PO Box 7710
Colorado Springs, CO 80933-7710

Editor: Theodore O. Zapel
Assistant editor: Audrey Scheck
Cover design: Jan Melvin

Library of Congress Cataloging-in-Publication Data

Cassady, Marsh, 1936-
  An introduction to—the art of theatre : a comprehensive text—past, present, and future / by Marsh Cassady.
    p. cm.
  ISBN-13: 978-1-56608-140-5 (pbk.)
  ISBN-10: 1-56608-140-8 (pbk.)
  1. Theater. I. Title. II. Title: Art of theatre.
  PN2037.C28 2006
  792–dc22
                      2006023624

1   2   3   07   08   09

Contents

Preface

An Introduction to: The Art of Theatre is written to be used for a one-semester introductory theatre course. Although the text is divided into Parts I-III, instructors may wish to take the parts in different order, emphasizing history over production, for example. Others may wish to deal with history only in passing. Any approach is workable. Even the order of chapters within various sections can be changed. For instance, some instructors may feel that the chapter on directing should come before the one on acting. The point is that the book is designed to work for you. Approach it however you like.

It is highly recommended that instructors assign the reading and discussion of plays for each section.

Using the Teacher's Guide

The guide is set up to correspond directly to the chapters in the book and serves as a resource for the instructor. For each chapter this manual provides the general learning goal or goals, along with the following:

Key Concepts: An outline of each chapter.

Additional Information: Background on selected concepts, themes, or individuals mentioned in the text.

Further Reading: A list of recommended plays that can be assigned to the entire class or to individual students.

Group Discussion Topics: Issues, questions, and critical thinking exercises beyond those in the text itself. These can be used to promote discussion in a large-class lecture setting or to provide review topics for small groups. Instructors even may choose to use the topics for chapter writing assignments.

Activities: Projects for self-guided learning.

Sample Exam Questions: True or false, multiple choice, fill in the blank, and short essay questions for each chapter. The instructor can tailor his or her own chapter examinations using some or all of the questions included in this manual. An answer key is provided at the end.

Part 1
THEATRE, DRAMA, AND PLACE

Chapter 1

WHAT ARE THEATRE AND DRAMA?

The goal for this chapter is twofold: to define theatre and to define drama.

Key Concepts

- Theatre is one of the oldest of the arts.

- In its close approximation to life, theatre relieves a sense of otherness.

- Theatre communicates a message, often more specifically than other arts.

- Theatre is more encompassing than many of the arts and often is more personally involving.

- Unlike many other arts, theatre exists in performance for only a limited time and never again can be presented in exactly the same manner.

- Theatre is unique in that it directly imitates human experience by allowing spectators to identify with characters who are represented as real.

- Theatre interprets life.

- Theatre encompasses many art forms.

- Theatre probably had its beginnings in two basic human traits: the mimetic instinct and the need for ritual.

- Theatre is like everyday life in that it involves ritual, pretense, imitation, and role playing.

- Theatre is in a constant state of change.

- To have lasting value, a play must possess universality. That is, it must deal with common feelings and beliefs.

- Theatre imitates but heightens life's experiences.

- A play is a basic plan for communicating with an audience.

- Aristotle believed a tragedy should be complete in itself and should contain everything necessary to its understanding.

- Aristotle defined what he believed to be the six basic elements of tragedy. They are plot, character, thought, dialog, melody, and spectacle.

- A theatrical production needs a balance between empathy and aesthetic distance so the audience can identify with the characters but still retain some detachment.

- Theatre employs many conventions or shortcuts as a way to expedite performances. These apply to writing, acting, and production.

Additional Information

To introduce Chapter 1, you may have students make arrangements to see a play, one that is currently being produced at the university theatre or perhaps at a community theatre. You may also consider showing a videotape of a play, either one of those mentioned in this chapter or one of your own choosing.

- Aristotle (384–322 BC) was a Greek philosopher and scientist whose *Poetics* analyzes the function and structural principles of tragedy (a second book, written on comedy, is lost). Aristotle argues that tragedy represents serious action and arouses terror and pity, leaving the spectator purged and strengthened.

- The protagonist was the chief, and at first the only, actor in Greek tragedy (He was originally the leader of the dithyrambs). Contemporary scholars use the term protagonist to mean the character whose choices move the play forward.

Further Reading

It is recommended that students read these two plays:

- *Death of a Salesman*
- *Oedipus Rex*

In addition, students may opt to read and report on or write about any of the other plays mentioned in Chapter 1.

Group Discussion Topics

- What makes theatre different from music, dance, or visual arts?
- Describe what is meant by universality in relation to a play.
- Give an example of a time when you played a role in order to get something from someone else.
- Describe a ritual you participate in on a regular basis. What do you gain by your participation?

- Read *Oedipus Rex* and discuss the various theatre conventions that would be necessary for the audience to willingly suspend their disbelief.
- Examine *Oedipus Rex* according to Aristotle's ideas of the structure of tragedy. How does the play fit his structure?

Activities

- In small groups, students should select a ritual that they can act out for the rest of the class. Each group should cast actors in the required roles and rehearse the playing out of the ritual prior to performance.
- Read one of the plays mentioned in Chapter 1. Cast and stage a scene from the play. Rehearse and memorize the dialog. Finally, present the scene for the class.
- Create a visual chart demonstrating how the plot line of *Oedipus Rex* fits Aristotle's theory for tragedy.
- Prepare for presentation in class a scene from one of the plays mentioned in Chapter 1. Present the scene, using the following acting conventions:
  - Project so that the audience can hear you.
  - Remember to position yourself so that the audience can see all of your actions.
  - Use gestures to communicate your feelings.
- Create a costume design for *Oedipus Rex*.
- Create a shoe-box model of the set you would like to use for a production of *Death of a Salesman*.

Chapter 1 Exam Questions

True or False   *Circle the correct answer.*

1. Any play can be considered universal.

    True   False

2. Human beings use imitation to help them achieve certain goals.

    True   False

3. Aristotle's theories should apply to all plays.

    True   False

4. A soliloquy is a speech by a character thinking out loud, revealing his or her innermost thoughts.

    True   False

Multiple Choice   *Circle the correct answer.*

1. A play with universality deals with:

    a. common feelings and beliefs.

    b. universal happiness.

    c. people from many cultures.

    d. every emotion taking place at once.

    e. none of the above.

2. Stock characters usually:

    a. remind us of ourselves.

    b. are always tragic.

    c. are always comedic.

    d. have highly exaggerated traits.

3. The term "closet drama" refers to:

    a. plays that are lost.

    b. performances of plays.

    c. plays performed in closets.

    d. plays written to be read, not performed.

    e. all of the above.

4. Aristotle was a(n):
   a. playwright.
   b. actor.
   c. philosopher.
   d. set designer.
   e. none of the above.

5. Dramatic time refers to:
   a. the length of a show.
   b. how long the audience will suspend their disbelief.
   c. how long it takes to tell a story.
   d. the amount of time represented by a play.
   e. all of the above.

Fill in the Blank

1. Theatre closely approximates _____.

2. The concept of _____ refers to the isolation an individual feels.

3. Because theatre exists only for a certain period of time, it is considered to be _____.

4. A play becomes unbelievable when the playwright deviates from the _____ or world that has been created.

5. An on-stage living room can be created by erecting a series of _____ positioned to represent the walls of a room.

Short Essay   *Use additional paper if necessary.*

1. In the process of imitating life, theatre often interprets it as well. Discuss how this interpretation comes about during the production process.

2. Since theatre reflects society, give an example of a recent play, TV show, or movie that you have seen that reflects the society in which you live. Give examples of the political, social, religious, or economic situation reflected in the production.

3. Describe the six elements Aristotle felt were essential for tragedy.

4. Discuss what is meant by "willingness to suspend disbelief."

5. What did Tennessee Williams mean when he referred to the script as "hardly more than an architect's blueprint of a house not yet built"?

Chapter 2
DRAMATIC STRUCTURE

The goal for this chapter is to provide a basic understanding of the various forms of dramatic structure.

Key Concepts

- Throughout history the story play has been written and produced more than any other type.
- The "story" in a story play encompasses everything that has happened in the world of the play before, during, and after the events of the plot.
- A frame of reference (framework) provides all the conditions of the world and universe of the play.
- Once a framework is established, a playwright cannot change it and hope to keep an audience's attention.
- Exposition or background information provides everything necessary for understanding a play.
- Most exposition is presented through the dialog, the rest through sets, lighting, costuming, and sometimes makeup.
- Exposition should not intrude on the progression of the play or call attention to itself.
- Story plays involve a clash of wills or forces between the protagonist and the antagonist.
- The protagonist most often is an individual.
- The antagonist can be a person, a group, or a nonindividualized force.
- Plots can involve four general types of conflict. They are the protagonist against: another person, self, society, or the forces of nature or fate.
- A basic plot involves an inciting incident, rising action, a turning point, a climax, and falling action.
- All the characters in a play have a goal they are trying to reach.

- There are several types of central problems. They are: the need for revenge; being lured by money, sex, or fame; the need to escape from an intolerable situation; not knowing which of two or more choices to make; and testing the limits of self and/or others.
- Scenes or divisions within an act can be thought of as either motivational units or French scenes.
- Beats are points of emphasis within scenes. With each, the action intensifies.
- Playwrights often imply rather than stating things openly.
- Thematic structure presents a series of scenes dealing with a basic issue but unrelated in continuity or character.
- Circular structure starts and ends with a similar set of circumstances.
- Ritualistic structure follows a pattern or structure over and over again.
- Episodic structure expands rather than condenses.

Additional Information

- Peter Brook is a British director who had a long association with the Royal Shakespeare Company. Influenced by Antonin Artaud and Bertolt Brecht, he integrated shock tactics as well as analytical calm and his own interpretation of these extremes in all of his productions. His most famous work was the telling of the religious epic *The Mahabharata* in 1985.
- Antonin Artaud was a French poet, actor, director, and theoretician. His *Theatre and Its Double* stressed the idea that theatre should not be mere entertainment but should ignite genuine action with real effects on the world.

Further Reading

The following are recommended. However, it would be difficult to read all of these in a short time period. So the student can perhaps choose one or two.

- *The Importance of Being Earnest* — For examples of exposition.
- *Wine in the Wilderness* — For universality.
- *The Bald Soprano* or *Waiting for Godot* — As examples of circular structure.

Students may also want to read other plays mentioned in the chapter. If they do, perhaps they can report on the plays or even present short excerpts from them in class.

Group Discussion Topics

- Which sort of play do you think you would prefer to see, an absurdist drama like *The Bald Soprano* or *Waiting for Godot*, or a realistic play such as *The Importance of Being Earnest*? Why?

- What is the most nonrealistic TV series you've watched recently? What makes it nonrealistic?

Activities

- Create a picture or story board that contains visual references to the political, social, and cultural world in Thornton Wilder's play *Our Town*.

- Divide into small groups and plan out the plot for a play. Take into consideration the "story," as well as the plot. Figure out everything you need to know about the background of the characters, the time, the environment and so on.

- Consider a major incident in your life and improvise a scene to share the incident. Carefully think through and justify your point of attack.

- Read a play discussed or mentioned in the chapter. Analyze the structure of that play. In which category discussed in this chapter does it fit?

Chapter 2 Exam Questions

True or False   *Circle the correct answer.*

1. The inciting incident and the climax of a play are often the same.
   True   False

2. Action is important in revealing character.
   True   False

3. Shakespeare's subplots often involved love and intrigue.
   True   False

4. Beats are the same as an actor's superobjective.
   True   False

5. In plays, people never speak through implication.
   True   False

Multiple Choice   *Circle the correct answer.*

1. Frame of reference is:
   a. the research done by the playwright before writing a script.
   b. the conditions of the world in which the play is set.
   c. the familial relationship of one character to another.
   d. a type of play done on a proscenium stage.
   e. none of the above.

2. The elements of a plot are:
   a. the inciting incident, rising action, turning point, climax, and denouement.
   b. character, place, action, and time.
   c. lights, costumes, sets, and makeup.
   d. superobjective, scenes, French scenes, and beats.
   e. none of the above.

3. The absurdist theatre often featured:
   a. musicals.
   b. circular plays.
   c. historical plays.
   d. story plays.
   e. all of the above.

4. An example of a central problem might be:
   a. greed.
   b. the lure of money.
   c. adultery.
   d. revenge.
   e. all of the above.

Fill in the Blank

1. A _____ is marked by the entrance and exit of a main character.

2. The _____ has the type of structure that is most often written and produced.

3. The _____ is the high point of the play.

4. _____ expands more than condenses.

5. The _____ is the point at which all the loose ends are tied up.

Short Essay   *Use additional paper if necessary.*
1. What is a story play?

2. What questions must be answered by a playwright when creating the frame of reference for a play?

3. What are the four general types of conflict or opposition found within plays?

4. List and give examples of the elements of plot in Arthur Miller's *Death of a Salesman*.

5. Define and discuss three different types of plot structure.

Chapter 3

DRAMATIC STYLE AND GENRE

The primary goal for this chapter is to explain the dramatic genres and styles.

Key Concepts

- Theatrical styles fall into two overall categories, the representational and the presentational. The former leans toward the realistic, the latter toward the nonrealistic. Specific styles are offshoots of representational and presentational theatre.

- The representational style is stage-centered, presenting dialog, setting, characters, and action as true to life.

- Presentational theatre is audience-centered. It says that theatre may come from life but should not be depicted as life.

- With naturalism, an attempt is made to include everything found in real life.

- Realism attempts to present life as it is, but selectively, without all the details.

- Expressionism attempts to show the protagonist's inner self.

- Symbolism tries to present truth subjectively or allegorically.

- With impressionism, the director and designer call attention to what they feel is important regarding the play's theme.

- Theatricalism, formalism, and constructivism are not styles in themselves, but are treatments of styles.

- Genre refers to the manner in which playwrights classify their subject matter.

- The purest form for serious treatment of a theme is tragedy.

- The purpose of tragedy is to teach us and to make us feel. In fact, there should be a catharsis, a purging of emotions which leaves us with a sense of tranquility.

- Tragedy is concerned with grandeur of ideas, theme, characters, and action.

- The workings of the protagonist's mind are the most important aspects of a tragedy.

- Historically, tragedy has dealt with characters of noble birth, but in modern times the characters are not necessarily highborn.
- Comedy usually makes us laugh at ourselves and our institutions. It has the most variety of the dramatic genres.
- Most comedies exaggerate traits, situations, and characters.
- The humor in most comedy often comes from showing a deviation from the norm, and often deals with eccentricities.
- Theatre of the absurd deals with a deviation of society, rather than of the individual.
- Comic devices include exaggeration, incongruity, automatism, character inconsistency, surprise, and derision.
- There are many types of comedies, but all can be classified as either high or low. The former uses verbal wit, while the latter uses physical humor.
- The primary purpose of farce is to entertain. Thus, the appeal is broad, and it takes little effort to follow the plot.
- Farce uses stock characters who are one-dimensional. Plots are contrived and rely on physical actions and devious twists. Many farces are concerned with illicit sex.
- Melodrama, like tragedy, treats a serious subject.
- The characters in traditional melodrama are one-dimensional, either all good or all bad.
- The plot in melodrama is contrived and filled with sensationalism. Good always triumphs.
- Modern melodrama most often is more realistic than that of the eighteenth and nineteenth centuries.
- Tragicomedy is a mingling of the serious and the comic, making it one of the most difficult genres since the playwright must advance the plot without totally confusing the audience.
- Many modern plays defy classification.

Additional Information

- Eric Bentley was a British-born drama critic, translator, editor, playwright, educator, and director. He gained recognition in the 1940s for his translations of Brecht's plays.
- Sophie Treadwell was one of the first female war correspondents. From 1916 to 1918, Ms. Treadwell turned to playwriting. Although she wrote several plays, *Machinal* is the best known. The play tells the story of a young woman who kills her husband and is sent to the electric chair. The play is loosely based on the real-life Snyder-Gray

murder trial, which occurred in 1926 and is an example of expressionism.

- William Butler Yeats was an Irish playwright who celebrated Irish culture in his plays. Yeats rejected the popular realism of his day, preferring to work with simple, suggestive sets. He often employed dance, music, and masks to tell his stories.
- Harold Pinter is a British actor, director, and playwright. He is considered an absurdist writer. From his work the term *Pinteresque* was coined, meaning anything menacing and enigmatic.

Further Reading

- *The Universal Wolf* — Constantly reminding spectators they are in a theatre. The play can be found in the book *Women on the Verge: Seven Avant Garde Plays*, edited by Rosette C. Lamont and published in 1993 by Applause Books.
- *The Happy Hunter* — A good example of farce.

Group Discussion Topics

- What are the two basic styles of theatre, and what makes them different?
- What makes a production naturalistic?
- Define impressionism.
- Discuss the ways in which *Death of a Salesman* shows a mingling of styles.
- What is the difference between style and genre?

Activities

- Write and perform a representational scene.
- Write and perform a presentational scene.
- Make two wall displays. The first should list all those plays you have read that fit the representational style, the second should list those plays that fit the presentational style. Allow your classmates to list plays they have read.
- Analyze a contemporary tragedy in terms of Aristotle's definition of tragedy. Does the play fit the mold? Why or why not?

Chapter 3 Exam Questions

True or False   *Circle the correct answer.*

1. All plays can be defined as comedy or tragedy.

   True   False

2. Tragedy does not allow us to maintain our faith in ourselves as a part of the human race.

   True   False

3. Comedy is often used to point out a social injustice.

   True   False

4. There is no limit to the subject matter used for comedy.

   True   False

5. Satire is generally used for the purposes of reform.

   True   False

Multiple Choice   *Circle the correct answer.*

1. Derision is:

   a. the mocking of people and institutions.

   b. the point in a tragedy when characters argue over what is right.

   c. a device used in tragedies.

   d. a character trait that shocks the audience.

   e. none of the above.

2. There are basically two types of comedy:

   a. comedic and tragic.

   b. burlesque and comedy of manners.

   c. high and low.

   d. repetitive or physical.

   e. none of the above.

3. In representational theatre the dialog, setting, characters, and action are:
    a. always comedic.
    b. usually stock characters.
    c. examples of postmodernism.
    d. true to life.
    e. all of the above.

4. Expressionism is a form of theatre that:
    a. is always tragic.
    b. is always representational.
    c. shows the protagonist's inner self.
    d. is based in realism.
    e. none of the above.

5. Theatricalism, formalism, and constructivism are:
    a. treatments of other styles.
    b. all types of tragicomedy.
    c. forms of naturalism.
    d. all necessary for a tragedy to be successful.
    e. all of the above.

Fill in the Blank

1. _____ has highly contrived plots.

2. In comedy, the protagonist always _____.

3. Farce has _____who are often one-dimensional.

4. The two categories of theatrical style presented in the chapter are _____.

Short Essay   *Use additional paper if necessary.*
1. Give examples of both high and low comedy. Justify your choices.

2. What did Aristotle say must be present in order for a play to be considered a tragedy?

3. What is the purpose of tragedy?

Chapter 4

ARCHITECTURE AND SPACE

The primary goal of this chapter is to explain how various styles of architecture and various spaces are used for creating theatrical events.

Key concepts

- Nearly any sort of space, if it's large enough, can accommodate theatre.
- The type of theatre structure affects audience expectations.
- The theatre building can be divided into two distinct parts, the "player area" and the "audience area."
- The player (or private) area includes the acting space and the spaces that support it — dressing rooms, scene shops, and storage areas. The public area comprises the auditorium, the lobby, and any other areas the spectators can enter.
- Theatre also can be separated into the performance area; the performance support areas, the audience areas, and the administrative areas.
- Theatre takes four basic structures: proscenium, arena stage, thrust stage, and found space.
- Proscenium theatre, the most traditional, has an arch that frames the action on-stage.
- Setting can be portrayed more realistically on a proscenium stage.
- Various types of setting can be used in a proscenium theatre. These include the box set, the drop, the wing and drop, and the wagon stage.
- Stage areas refer back to the Renaissance when stages were sloped upward from front to back. Upstage is the area closest to the back wall. Stage Right is the actors' right as they face the audience. From these all other areas can be determined.
- Proscenium staging has a number of advantages: more special effects are possible; the front curtain can be closed to mask changes and signal the end of an act; settings and set pieces can be brought on-stage more easily; actors can wait just off-stage to make their entrances.

- A disadvantage to the proscenium theatre is the physical and psychological separation of actor and audience.
- Directors and actors in a proscenium theatre need to be constantly aware of sightlines.
- In arena staging, the audience surrounds the action, which generally is lower than the seating area.
- Although scenery for an arena theatre cannot be as realistic as that for a proscenium stage, the properties, costumes, and makeup must be more realistic since the audience is closer to the actors.
- There are problems of concealment in an arena theatre, and the director cannot be so concerned with presenting an aesthetically pleasing picture. Rather, the director must be more concerned that all of the audience will be able to see most of the action.
- Advantages of arena staging are that the audience is closer to the actors, there is no physical barrier, and almost any room or space can be adapted for arena staging.
- A thrust stage consists of an open playing area similar to that of an arena theatre, with a stagehouse or wall in the background through which performers enter and exit. Because of the back wall and stagehouse, more scenery can be used than is possible in arena theatre.
- Audiences are close to the action in a thrust stage theatre.
- A variation to the thrust stage is the end stage.
- Various other types of stages are variations of the proscenium, the arena, and the thrust stages.
- A black box is a theatre that contains a flexible staging area which allows for various staging and seating arrangements.
- Environmental theatre involves adapting whatever space is available to a theatrical production.
- The backstage area in a theatre should be much larger than the playing area.
- A theatre also needs areas for lighting control, costuming, set and properties construction, and for makeup and dressing.

Additional Information

The Performance Group was one of the most controversial and visible of the environmental theatre groups of the 1960s and 1970s. It was formed by Richard Schechner, the critic, director, and editor of the *Drama Review*. The group was known for its risk taking, concern for social issues, and investigation of ritual.

Group Discussion Topics

- What kinds of theatre structures exist in the area where you live? What sorts of plays are produced in each?
- Discuss the advantages and disadvantages of each type of theatre structure.
- What theatre structure do you think would best suit the following plays: *Death of a Salesman, Our Town, Waiting for Godot?*

Activities

- Tour a local theatre and identify the four categories of spaces as you visit them.
- Create a model of an ideal theatre building. You may wish to include multiple playing spaces. Budget is not an issue.
- After creating your ideal theatre building, plan a potential season. Remember that different types of plays work better in certain spaces.
- Make a model for a box set that could be used for *The Glass Menagerie.*
- Do some additional research on the environmental theatre that was popular during the 1960s. Report your findings to the class.

Chapter 4 Exam Questions

True or False   *Circle the correct answer.*

1. Specific illumination refers to all the lights on-stage.

    True   False

2. The most traditional type of theatre is the proscenium stage.

    True   False

3. Sets built on proscenium stages do not suggest the existence of a fourth wall.

    True   False

4. Stage Left is the actor's left as he or she faces the audience.

    True   False

5. Almost any room or space can be adapted to arena staging.

    True   False

Multiple Choice   *Circle the correct answer.*

1. The following is a type of theatre space:
    a. proscenium.
    b. black box.
    c. thrust.
    d. arena.
    e. all of the above.

2. The staging for an arena-style production would:
    a. be a box set.
    b. have the audience seated on three sides.
    c. use teasers and tormentors to mask the lighting instruments.
    d. always be concerned with picturization.
    e. have the audience surrounding the action on all sides.

3. Work lights are used:
   a. to illuminate the audience.
   b. to illuminate the set during a show.
   c. to illuminate the administrative areas of the theatre.
   d. none of the above.

4. The term *open stage* refers to:
   a. a theatre that is open to the public.
   b. the actors perform in a large open space rather than in one that is small and cramped.
   c. having a unified space that contains the audience area and the acting area.
   d. a box set that is open due to the removal of the fourth wall.
   e. all of the above.

Fill in the Blank

1. Upstage is the area _____ from the audience.

2. A stage that has the audience seated on three sides of the playing space is called a _____.

3. The type of scenery most often used to suggest the interior walls of a room is _____.

4. A _____ stage also is called a picture frame stage.

5. The area behind the top of the arch and above the stage in a proscenium theatre is called _____.

Short Essay   *Use additional paper if necessary.*

1. List the advantages and disadvantages of the four styles of theatre structure discussed in the chapter.

2. What is a wagon stage? What are its advantages?

3. How may a revolving stage be used?

4. Why are stage floors made of soft pine?

Part II
THE PRODUCTION

Chapter 5
THE PLAYWRIGHT

The primary goal for this chapter is to explain the role of the playwright.

Key Concepts

- In most cases, the playwright, working alone, begins the creative process that results in a production before an audience.
- In order to assimilate a diversity of material into a production, a dramatist needs to be acquainted with the various areas of theatre.
- Most theatrical productions involve one person's script to which others add their interpretations.
- Ideas for plays can come from anywhere. Once playwrights have an initial idea they often add to it in the following ways:
    - They examine something important or relevant in their lives.
    - They examine their feelings.
    - They choose to write about something that arouses their curiosity.
    - They choose a haunting subject or situation.
    - They begin with a real person, current or historical.
    - They begin with a set of circumstances.
    - They begin with a setting.
    - They adapt a play from another medium.
- Most playwrights choose a certain type of audience for their plays.
- There has to be common ground where the playwright and the audience meet.
- Playwrights need a balance in their work between what is common to all of us and what is unique to the individual.
- The most memorable element of most plays is the characters.
- After developing the characters, a playwright needs to decide what parts of them an audience should see.
- A character has to want something, which he or she then tries to get.
- There are various ways of revealing character, but the most important is seeing him or her in action.

- Dialog has three main functions: to reveal character, to create atmosphere, and to advance the plot.
- Physical activity can sometimes be more effective than dialog in revealing character or advancing the plot.
- Most writers have some sort of an idea about the progression of events, the theme, or even the resolution of a play before putting words on paper.
- A play needs to hook the audience's attention immediately.
- There are various ways of presenting exposition. Some are through using a narrator, using flashbacks, having characters talk about another character, and through scenery, costuming, and lighting.
- A script often takes many drafts before it is finished.
- It is difficult to have a play produced.
- There are workshops, various types of theatres, and organizations that help a playwright develop a script.
- Playwrights have the choice of submitting their work to producers; contests; professional, educational, community, and summer theatres; agents; and drama publishers.

Additional Information

Michael Weller (1942–) is an American playwright whose popular work *Moonchildren* won him critical acclaim when it opened on the Arena Stage in 1971, followed by successful Broadway and Off-Broadway productions. He is also known for writing the screenplay of the 1979 movie *Hair*.

Further Reading

- *My Sister in this House* — A play based loosely on a real event.
- *Long Day's Journey Into Night* or *Three Tall Women* — Plays based on the playwrights' own families.
- *Painting Churches* — Learning to know the characters by their actions and personalities.

Group Discussion Topics

- Discuss a historical or current event that would be an interesting subject for a play.
- Discuss the major characters of a particular play, such as *Our Town* or *Othello*. What are their universal traits? What are their idiosyncrasies?

- Which playwright whose work you've encountered so far in the course is your favorite? Why?
- In what way is playwriting a collaborative art?
- If you were to write a play, what sort of audience would you want to attend its production? Why?

Activities

- Write a one-act play. Cast and perform the play for your class.
- Using your favorite short story, take on the role of playwright and adapt the work for the stage.
- Investigate the life and performances of Danny Hock.
- Read Tina Howe's *Painting Churches* and determine the major goals of the parents and the daughter.

Chapter 5 Exam Questions

True or False   *Circle the correct answer.*

1. Playwrights sometimes attempt to reinforce common beliefs.

    True   False

2. Exposition happens only after the climax of the play.

    True   False

3. Physical actions can be more effective than dialog in revealing information about a character.

    True   False

Multiple Choice   *Circle the correct answer.*

1. Ideas for plays often come from:

    a. things relevant to the playwright.

    b. the playwright's life.

    c. curiosity about a subject.

    d. real people.

    e. all of the above.

2. A playwright's first decision must be:

    a. why the playwright wants to write the play and whom he or she wants to reach.

    b. who are the characters and what are their goals?

    c. where will the play take place and what is the situation?

    d. exposition.

    e. none of the above.

3. An audience will accept a play:

    a. only if they are familiar with the cultural and social background of the characters.

    b. if it is centered neither on the human condition nor the individual characters.

    c. if the ideas and situations are more important than the characters.

    d. as long as it deals with human problems and emotions.

    e. none of the above.

4. An audience is more likely to accept the theme of a play if:
    a. they are in at least partial agreement with it.
    b. the characters are likable.
    c. they do not have to relate the action on-stage to their own lives.
    d. the characters are not fully developed.
    e. all of the above.

5. Dialog should:
    a. create atmosphere.
    b. reveal character.
    c. advance the plot.
    d. be clear, appropriate, and natural.
    e. all of the above.

Fill in the Blank

1. The most memorable element of the majority of plays is _____.

2. A scene that jumps backward in time to portray a particular event is called a _____.

3. Progressive exposition is related to the unfolding of the plot and the _____ of the characters.

Short Essay   *Use additional paper if necessary.*
1. List three criteria for good dialog.

2. List at least three techniques for presenting exposition.

3. Describe how a playwright can reveal information about a character.

4. Give an example of how physical activity might be used to give information about a character.

5. Describe ways in which a playwright might go about writing a play once he or she has determined the theme.

Chapter 6
THE ACTOR

The major goal of the chapter is to describe and explain the process of acting.

Key concepts

- The actor is the person with whom theatre audiences most closely identify.
- Actors have little but themselves to use as the instrument of their art.
- Unlike painters or writers who can revise what they do, actors have only a given moment to present their art to the spectator.
- Although roleplaying and acting both rely on the mimetic instinct, acting generally is more thought out and planned, and the actor is more aware of fitting into an overall scheme.
- To succeed, an actor must have determination and be willing to undergo endless training and years of work.
- The actors' major tools are the mind, the body, and the voice. Actors must be acquainted with and understand various acting techniques and styles of production and how to execute these styles.
- An actor should be in good physical shape to meet the demands of roles that can call for many sorts of physical activities.
- Actors need to develop their voices to the highest potential.
- Although actors undergo formal training under the supervision of teachers, much of their development involves self-training. This means getting outside of themselves and observing the world around them.
- Actors need to let the imagination soar and not be afraid to experiment with various ways of portraying a role.
- An actor's creativity often is intuitive in creating an illusion that suggests reality to an audience.
- Actor training involves many areas such as oral interpretation, singing, dancing, fencing and often team sports.
- Actors often are asked to create scenes and roles from given circumstances (exposition) that set up a scene. They also may do exercises involving sense memory — remembering and portraying anything sensory.

- Actors also may participate in sensitivity training.
- Actors need to be acquainted with the areas of the stage and how to use them effectively.
- Actors need to be able to perform in a variety of styles.
- Unlike sculptors or painters, for instance, actors collaborate with others, and so have a duty to the designers, the director, the other actors, the playwright, and the audience.
- Overall, there are two major approaches to acting, the internal and the external. The internal — as first put together by Stanislavsky — involves approaching a role from the viewpoint of emotions, the subconscious, and the natural. It looks to life itself for developing a role. The external approach is largely concerned with technique, though the technique of portraying a particular emotion often bring about feelings associated with the way of doing things ... such as smiling and then beginning to feel in a positive mood.
- Other approaches to acting were developed by the Living Theatre of Julian Beck and Judith Malina, who sought to make drama fluid and poetic, and Jerzy Grotowski, who proclaimed the need for discipline and spontaneity. Grotowski said the actor should not need sets, makeup, lighting, or costuming to believably portray a role.
- Involved in developing a character is the need to analyze a role by finding the superobjective (in realistic plays) and the specific objective for each scene.
- Actors try to determine as much as possible about each character they are to portray. This involves the character's personality, background, and perspectives. Next they decide which traits are most important to show an audience. Then they determine relationships to other characters.
- A character is not analyzed and determined all at once but continues to grow throughout the rehearsal period.
- Actors need to memorize not only their own lines and business but their cues so they know when to respond. They must be willing, when necessary, to subjugate themselves to the overall ensemble.
- Good acting has the appearance of spontaneity.
- In portraying a role, an actor has to balance the artistic against the technical.
- It is extremely difficult to make a living as an actor.

Additional Information

- The Moscow Art Theatre was founded in 1898 by Constantin Stanislavsky and Vladimir Nemirovich-Danchenko. The theatre was dedicated to the highest ideals of ensemble art, good citizenship, and public education. The company strived for naturalness, simplicity, and clarity in their work, in direct contrast to the declamatory acting popular at the time.

- The Living Theatre was founded by Julian Beck and his wife Judith Malina in 1948. They began the trend toward Off-Off-Broadway productions with one of the most influential and longest-lasting avant-garde theatres in America. The theatre and its founders were the leaders of the experimental theatre movement of the 1960s.

Further Reading

- *Towards A Poor Theatre* by Jerzy Grotowski
- *An Actor Prepares* by Constantin Stanislavsky

Group Discussion Topics

- What is the difference between the internal and external approach to acting?
- Why is it so difficult to make a living as an actor in this country?
- What is meant by the expression, "An actor's body and voice are the tools of his craft"?
- How does an actor go about creating a character?
- Why should someone continue studying once he or she has become a professional actor?

Activities

- Create a list of questions you would like to have answered if you were able to interview Willy or Linda in *Death of a Salesman* in order to learn more about his or her character.

- Read a play and then write a character biography for any one of the characters. Remember that you may invent facts about the character that are not specifically given by the playwright.

- Using the internal approach to acting, select and perform a monolog for class.

- Using the external approach to acting, select and perform a monolog for the class.

- Select a character from a play and do what you can to make yourself appear more physically similar to that character.

Chapter 6 Exam Questions

True or False   *Circle the correct answer.*

1. Constantin Stanislavsky was a founder of the Moscow Art Theatre.
   True   False

2. Nearly thirty percent of the members of Actors' Equity Association are employed as actors at any given time.
   True   False

3. Actors must be able to communicate feeling by using their voices and bodies.
   True   False

4. The external approach to acting is largely concerned with technique.
   True   False

5. Most actors can make a living in any major city.
   True   False

6. Much of actor training involves self-training.
   True   False

Multiple Choice   *Circle the correct answer.*

1. An actor's major tools are:
   a. voice, body, mind, self.
   b. costumes, makeup, set, props.
   c. designers, technicians, directors.
   d. shoes, hats, purses, canes.
   e. none of the above.

2. Actors must use their imaginations to:
   a. figure out how to feel in a given situation.
   b. anticipate how a character would deliver a line.
   c. figure out how to react in a situation.
   d. fill in information not given by the playwright.
   e. all of the above.

3. When actors use sense memory:

    a. they rely on the sense of a scene to remember dialog.

    b. they are able to sense the moves of fellow actors.

    c. they use common sense in portraying characters.

    d. they call up and portray sensory memories.

    e. none of the above.

4. An actor's superobjective refers:

    a. to finding the character's goal.

    b. to objective analysis of the role.

    c. to being super objective when judging the rest of the cast.

    d. to choosing the correct objects to use as hand props.

    e. to the actors' continuous sense of self.

5. Stage business is:

    a. using the internal approach to acting.

    b. paying attention to your own character and not others' characters on the stage.

    c. physical action.

    d. related solely to the ensemble concept.

    e. a concept developed by Grotowski.

Fill in the Blank

1. Good acting should not _____ to itself.

2. The _____ is the theatre artist with whom the audience most closely identifies.

3. The Polish Laboratory Theatre was started by _____.

4. Directors often have actors _____to get the sense of a scene in their own vocabulary.

5. Actors' Equity Association is the _____ for actors in legitimate theatre.

Short Essay   *Use additional paper if necessary.*

1. Who was Constantin Stanislavsky? What were his major contributions to the theatre?

2. Who was Jerzy Grotowski? What were his major contributions to the theatre?

3. Describe the two major approaches to acting.

4. Describe the actor's process in creating a role.

Chapter 7
THE DIRECTOR

The primary goal of this chapter is to explain what is involved in being a director, from selecting a script to casting a play and working with actors in rehearsals.

Key Concepts

- The director, who usually is the first theatre artist involved in bringing a production to life before an audience, has a myriad of duties, which differ depending on the type of theatre with which he or she is associated, and needs to be acquainted with all areas of production.

- In selecting scripts for production, directors need to be able to judge what will be acceptable to potential audiences and what sort of people are likely to attend the productions. The play needs to fit into the overall season. They can only make educated guesses about what will be successful.

- A director needs to analyze the script to determine what the writer means and how he or she meant to say it. This involves learning as much as possible about the writer and the context in which the play was written.

- Most directors work out most of their analysis before beginning rehearsals.

- A director's analysis of the script is similar to that of the actor, though inclusive of all the characters. In addition, directors need to determine which elements are most important for the audience's understanding of the play. They also need to determine plot elements, focus, and atmosphere. Most important, they need to do their best to be true to the playwright's original intent.

- During the analysis, a director also thinks in terms of setting and technical elements in determining how best to portray atmosphere, mood, actions, and circumstances. Yet there must be collaboration and compromise among director and designers in bringing the ideas to life.

- In casting the play, the director has to be a good judge of human behavior, as well as talent.

- There are various types of auditions. The most common are the open audition, where the actors all appear at the same time, and the interview, which is conducted one-on-one between actor and director. Each has distinct advantages and disadvantages.

- Rehearsal periods generally last from four weeks in professional theatre to six weeks in educational and community theatre. There are six stages.

  - Reading rehearsals have the purpose of coming to a clear understanding and interpretation of the play.

  - During blocking rehearsals the action, movement, and business are worked out to keep the play from appearing static and to give it life. The movement and business have to be motivated by the script, through supplementary business, that which enhances characterization or theme, while inherent business relies on such things as exits and entrances.

  - In character and line rehearsals, the performers develop and build their characters and try to discover the most effective method of delivering their speeches.

  - During finishing rehearsals, all the elements of acting are developed and unified.

  - Technical rehearsals are devoted to coordinating the visual and sound elements with the total production.

  - During dress rehearsals, the play ideally is given just as it will be in performance.

- The length of each type of rehearsal depends on several factors, including the actors' degrees of experience, the difficulty of performance, and special requirements such as singing and dancing.

- Many of the principles of directing are the same for arena theatre as proscenium, but there are differences, many involved with the need for detail since the audience generally is closer to the action. The director also has less control over picturization, and body position has little value since it is perceived differently from different areas of the audience. For the same reason, spacing also is unimportant. It is important that actors be open to most of the audience as much as possible. Movement can be more natural and less restrained, and levels, in most cases, are more important.

- Dramaturgs serve as literary managers and work closely with the director in researching a play's background and in analyzing and interpreting the script.

- The stage manager is second in command to the director and serves as liaison between cast/crew and management. It is this person's duty to see that the entire production continues as rehearsed.

- A choreographer plans and rehearses dance numbers for musicals. The preparation includes an analysis of the script similar to that done by the actor or director.

Additional Information

- Tyrone Guthrie (1900–1971) was a British director. Guthrie was an innovative and popular international director from the 1930s on. The Guthrie Theatre in Minneapolis was named for him. He directed Laurence Olivier in productions of *Hamlet* and *Henry V*. He is noted for having gained public acceptance for alternatives to the proscenium arch. Guthrie was knighted in 1961.

- José Quintero was born in Panama in 1924. He specialized in directing the plays of Eugene O'Neill. Quintero is noted for helping to launch the Circle in the Square Theatre in 1949. His autobiography, *If You Don't Dance, They Beat You*, was published in 1974.

- Harold Clurman (1901–1980) was an American director, critic, author, and teacher. As the founder and inspirational leader of the Group Theatre (1931–1940), he nurtured the talents of many young playwrights, including Clifford Odets and Irwin Shaw.

Group Discussion Topics

- List all the various responsibilities of a director preparing for a production.

- Discuss how a director might go about analyzing a script for production.

- Discuss the plays selected for a local professional or community theatre season. Do you think the season will succeed? Why?

- Discuss the various types of auditions and the pros and cons of each.

- After viewing a professional production, discuss the concept chosen by the director. Evaluate the director's success in realizing the concept throughout the production.

Activities

- Select a script and hold a mock audition to cast your classmates in the roles. Justify your choices.

- Plan a season for your school or a local community theatre. Justify your choices.

- Select a script and do additional research about the social, political, and economic environment of the time in which it was written or the historical period in which it is set.

- Do additional research about your favorite playwright and present the information to your class.
- As a group activity, arrange to interview a local director about his or her views of the directing process. If possible, attend one of the rehearsals of an upcoming production.

Chapter 7 Exam Questions

True or False *Circle the correct answer.*

1. A director does not need to have any knowledge of set design.

   True   False

2. Directors often look for a theme or metaphor for a particular show.

   True   False

3. The director's analysis of a play includes thinking in terms of setting and technical elements.

   True   False

4. In commercial more than educational theatre, the director must be a good judge of human behavior.

   True   False

Multiple Choice   *Circle the correct answer.*

1. The occupation of director stems in large part from practices instituted by:

   a. William Shakespeare.

   b. Off-Broadway productions.

   c. Edward Albee.

   d. the Duke of Saxe-Meiningen.

   e. the Living Theatre.

2. Directors sometimes designate areas of the stage to correspond to the face of a clock when:

   a. directing musicals.

   b. directing for an arena stage.

   c. directing for a thrust stage.

   d. directing for a proscenium stage.

   e. all of the above.

3. At auditions the director must consider:
   a. how easily actors move.
   b. the actors' emotional depth and range.
   c. the quality of their voices.
   d. their overall potential for a role.
   e. all of the above.

4. Blocking rehearsals are devoted to:
   a. blocking out the actors' motivational units.
   b. planning the technical elements.
   c. the actors having to block out all external distractions.
   d. unifying all the elements of a production.
   e. planning the action and business.

Fill in the Blank

1. Most business and movement is planned during _____ rehearsals.

2. In a _____ audition, the director meets one-on-one with the actors.

3. The final stage of the rehearsal period is called the _____.

4. Physical closeness on-stage often implies _____ closeness.

5. Pace, timing, and rhythm make up the three broad aspects of _____.

Short Essay   *Use additional paper if necessary.*

1. Discuss the ways a director might work with the designers in determining an overall design scheme.

2. What should a director consider when trying to cast a play?

3. What should a director take into consideration when analyzing a play?

4. Discuss how a director might develop an overall production concept.

5. Name and describe six types of rehearsals.

Chapter 8

THE DESIGNERS AND SUPPORTING ARTISTS

The primary goal of this chapter is to have students understand the roles of the scene designer, the lighting designer, the costume designer, the makeup designer, the property manager, and the audio designer.

Key Concepts

- It is important for the director and designers to establish a good working relationship where there can be a free exchange of ideas.

- To design a practical and aesthetically pleasing set to match a variety of styles and historical periods, a designer needs training, experience, and talent in many different areas including carpentry, architecture, lighting, set construction, interior decorating, and the various theatrical styles.

- A set helps convey a play's theme and provides information essential to its understanding of the play. It fulfills the director's interpretation, provides an environment for the action, remains faithful to the playwright's intent, and complements the work of the other designers. It establishes both a framework for the action and a focal point for the audience, and it is designed for easy use by the actors.

- The set should present an aesthetically pleasing image and provide necessary exposition.

- The set should be balanced, either symmetrically or asymmetrically, and its element should be harmonious.

- Colors and shapes help convey style and genre.

- The work of designing a play begins with a study and analysis of the script to determine mood and theme and also to answer practical questions about such things as doors, windows, and fireplaces.

- A scene designer prepares preliminary sketches to show the director and later does a variety of other drawings. One of the more important of these is the floor plan, which shows the set in scale. A designer often does a scale model, as well.

- There are two categories of stage lighting: general and specific. The former provides a well-lighted performance area, while the second provides special effects.

- Light complements the other areas of design and helps convey the play's mood and message. It provides exposition and often is symbolic.

- Lighting consists of two components: a source and a system of control. The first refers to the lighting instruments, the second to the dimmer board or the panel from which the lights are controlled. The most common lighting instruments are spotlights and floodlights of which there are various types. The dimmer board allows the lighting technician to dim from one area to another and to control both the intensity of the light and the direction from which it originates. It provides control over color.

- Lighting designers work closely with the director and the other designers to bring to fruition the overall design concept. They know which lights to use for various effects and where to hang them for best results.

- Lighting designers plan control of three aspects of lighting: color, intensity, and distribution. They know that the first function of lighting is to provide selective visibility.

- A lighting designer prepares a light plot, which is a scale plan showing a mixture of general and specific lighting and an instrument schedule. This shows where each instrument is to be hung and focused. The designer also draws a lighting sectional which shows a composite side view of the location of the instruments and the set.

- Lighting designers divide the stage into areas, using a minimum of two instruments for specific illumination in each area. This is to eliminate long shadows and to light each side of the actor or set piece. They prepare a list of cues so the technician knows exactly what to change and when.

- The lighting and scene designer work closely together since what one does strongly affects the other.

- Costuming conveys a great deal of information about characters and their situations.

- The costume is the facet of design that most identifies and supports the character.

- Costume designers need a specialized background and a flair for style. They need to keep in mind the characters' motives and personalities and design the costumes accordingly. They must know how to create costumes that will support rather than hinder an actor's movement. The designs also have to be consistent with the production's overall concept.

- Costume designers need to be aware of color symbolism.

- In analyzing a script, the costume designer has to consider such things as place and time and the economic situation of the characters.

- A costume designer needs to have a comprehensive knowledge of texture and fabric.

- There are three categories of makeup: straight, stylized, and character. Straight makeup enhances or projects an actor's natural features. Stylized and Character makeup alter an actor's appearance. Stylized makeup is planned by a makeup designer so it meshes with the overall production style.

- Makeup designers need to be acquainted with the theory of color so they know what will look good under various colors of light.

- For special needs, makeup designers often prepare schematics, outlines of the head with the face divided into areas and planes. The designer uses these to indicate the color and special features of each area.

- The property master is responsible for determining, obtaining, and caring for all the properties of a production and then returning those that have been rented or borrowed once the show closes.

- The property master is responsible for determining where to get those props that can be procured and for designing and building those that are unavailable.

- During the run of a show, the property crew is responsible for the props being where they should be for easy access and that they are in good repair.

- There are three overall categories of props: set props include anything that stands within the set; set dressing includes such things as wall fixtures, paintings, vases, and figurines; hand props are those things the actors carry and can include objects they carry or handle on-stage.

- Properties add to a production's authenticity, augment characterization, and provide visual effects.

- The property master makes plots that list where props are to be placed and that show how props are to be shifted during blackouts or intermissions.

- Audio designers provide the sound effects and music for a play. To do this, they need to determine what sounds are necessary to give the play a sense of reality and to uphold the design concept. They need to know how a particular sound is used and why.

- The designer needs to be acquainted with where specific sound effects can be acquired.

- Audio designers know the effects of combinations of sounds and how to present them in accordance with the style of the production and the genre.

- The designers need to analyze a script to determine what sounds are needed and how they should be presented.

- With advanced technology, the use of sound for the theatre is becoming a sophisticated process.

- Theatre always has been a combination of forms, and in the present day is often a true mixture of forms including live presentation, video, computer graphics, and television.

- New technologies for the theatre are developing rapidly. They include various uses of computers and the World Wide Web. Another development is the use of projections for special effects or even to provide entire settings.

- Computer-aided design is becoming common for such areas as stage settings, costuming, and audio design.

- Robotic lights or color scrollers are now in wide use. Lights can automatically follow actors' movements and can provide spectacular color and dimming effects.

Additional Information

A basic understanding of color is necessary in almost all areas of design. Lighting designers especially must understand how light and color integrate and complement each other. As you discuss this chapter, you can cover the concept of color relationships by showing color wheels, which provide designers a schematic view of primary and secondary hue relationships as well as pairs of complementary colors that appear diametrically opposed to each other around the wheel.

Group Discussion Topics

- Discuss the skills necessary to be a scene designer.

- What are the primary responsibilities of a costume designer?

- What sort of things does the lighting designer look for in the analysis of the script?

- Why are accurate properties important to a production?

- Describe the responsibilities of a sound designer.

54

Activities

- Select a play and develop a light plot for a production.
- Select a play and develop a properties plot for a production.
- Select a play and draw preliminary costume sketches for a production.
- Select a play and draw preliminary sketches of the set design.
- Select a play and develop a sound plot for a production.

Chapter 8 Exam Questions

True or False   *Circle the correct answer.*

1. A designer may exaggerate an element of a setting to point out an aspect of the play.

   True   False

2. Lighting designers do not need a knowledge of electricity.

   True   False

3. The scenic elements should remain subordinate to the overall production.

   True   False

4. One function of lighting is to provide selective visibility.

   True   False

5. A costume designer must keep in mind the personality rather than the motives of any particular character.

   True   False

Multiple Choice   *Circle the correct answer.*

1. The sound designer must be concerned with:

   a. the source of a sound.

   b. the emotional and psychological content of the scene.

   c. the style and genre of the production.

   d. how sound effects can be acquired.

   e. all of the above.

2. A well-designed set should have:

   a. a variety of colors.

   b. a box set.

   c. asymmetrical balance.

   d. harmony and balance.

   e. none of the above.

3. Makeup designers often prepare schematics:
    a. to indicate a character's personality type.
    b. to indicate color and special features of each area of the face.
    c. to see if the costuming and makeup are of a similar hue.
    d. to teach the actors how to apply their makeup.
    e. none of the above.

4. Properties are important because they:
    a. add to a production's authenticity.
    b. direct attention to the actors.
    c. provide a focal point for the audience.
    d. direct attention to the actors' movements.
    e. expedite rapid scene changes.

5. The setting:
    a. provides an environment for the actors.
    b. complements the work of the other designers.
    c. helps convey the play's theme.
    d. helps fulfill the production's overall interpretation.
    e. all of the above.

Fill in the Blank

1. There are three styles of makeup. They are straight, stylized, and
    _____.

2. An object carried on-stage by an actor is called a _____.

3. A set with left and right halves that are exactly the same is
    _____.

4. Such things as wall fixtures, paintings, plaques, and vases used in a
    production are called _____.

Short Essay   *Use additional paper if necessary.*

1. Describe what is meant if a set has balance and harmony.

2. What are the purposes of floor plans and models?

3. In what ways is multimedia theatre being influenced by new technologies?

4. Where might a costume designer go to research period costumes?

Chapter 9
THE BUSINESS SIDE OF THEATRE

The primary goal for this chapter is to provide students with an understanding of how educational, community, and nonprofit theatres are run.

Key Concepts

- The producer can be an individual or a group. The manner of financing and the method of handling business arrangements depend on the type of theatre.

- In educational theatre, the school itself, or a department of the school, is the producer. Money may be advanced by the school or by an organization in the school. In community theatre, a board of directors approves expenditures.

- The important consideration for educational theatre is to plan a balanced season, whereas community theatre's major concern is selecting plays that draw well.

- More and more professional theatres of various types have been established throughout the United States in recent decades.

- Until the late 1960s or early 70s, most professional theatre existed to make a profit. Then the change to nonprofit regional theatres changed the face of professional theatre.

- Subsidized theatre, with itself as producer, theoretically allows more freedom in choice of plays.

- Rising costs have made Broadway theatre a risky venture. Most plays are presented to appeal to a mass audience. The producer is concerned largely with staging a show that will be a hit.

- Off-Broadway theatre, as defined by Actors' Equity Association, seats no more than 299 audience members. There need not be so great a concern about staging a hit show. Occasionally, Off-Broadway shows are so successful that they move to Broadway.

- For most Off-Broadway and Broadway shows, a producer takes an option on a play. The producer then is responsible for raising money to stage the show and for making all the financial arrangements, including the renting of rehearsal space and a theatre.

- Producers have no direct working arrangement with the artistic end of a play, but they approve any alterations since these affect the show's audience-drawing potential. They also are responsible for advertising.

- In recent years promotion and publicity has taken the form of "event marketing," largely due to Canadian producer Garth Drabinsky.

- The Disney Company also is having a big impact on Broadway with hits like *Beauty and the Beast* and *The Lion King*.

- A producer's final responsibility is deciding when to end a show's run.

- A solution to Broadway's financial difficulties is to have a closer relationship among nonprofit and commercial theatres.

- The business staff of a theatre includes a general manager and a company manager. The former negotiates agreements with the director, the theatre owners, the designers, and the lead performers. The general manager develops the production budget.

- The company manager is the producer's representative in the day-to-day business operations of a production.

- The house manager supervises such staff members as ushers, doormen, and cleaners, as well as checking box office statements and overseeing house maintenance.

- Publicity managers and press agents are responsible for selling tickets, for projecting a good image of the theatre, and for publicizing the show.

Additional Information

- The American Repertory Theatre was founded in Boston in 1980 by Robert Bruestein, in association with Harvard University. (The first theatre to be known by this name was founded in 1946, but it disbanded in 1948.) The company is dedicated to neglected works from the past, innovative classical productions, and new American plays. In 1986 ART received a special Tony award and a National Endowment for the Arts Ongoing Ensemble Award. In 1987, the theatre began the Institute for Advanced Theatre Training.

- The Goodman Theatre, located in Chicago, is the country's second-oldest regional theatre. Founded in 1925 alongside the Art Institute of Chicago, the theatre was to house both a resident professional company and a school of drama. The professional company did not survive the Great Depression, but the school continued.

Group Discussion Topics

- Why is Broadway theatre said to be in a "crisis period"?
- Discuss the benefits of being a nonprofit theatre company.
- Discuss the role of the producer for Broadway companies.
- If you were named publicity manager of the next school production, what strategies might you use to attract an audience?
- How do you think Broadway should try to solve its financial problems?

Activities

- Interview the producer of a local theatre company. Ask about the financial aspects of running the theatre.
- Prepare a sample budget for a production at your school or community theatre.
- Volunteer to usher at a community or school theatrical performance.
- Make a chart of the stage manager's responsibilities.

Chapter 9 Exam Questions

True or False   *Circle the correct answer.*

1. The producer's job is finished once a director is hired.

   True   False

2. Broadway theatre is currently experiencing a time of great prosperity.

   True   False

3. Regional theatre is supported in large part by grants.

   True   False

4. Nonprofit theatre was more common in the first half of the twentieth century.

   True   False

5. The main factor in determining whether a theatre is designated as Off-Broadway is size.

   True   False

Multiple Choice   *Circle the correct answer.*

1. In educational theatre, plays are produced by:

   a. private organizations.

   b. a department of the school.

   c. the house and box office staff.

   d. the drama teacher.

   e. none of the above.

2. In theatrical productions, the term *angels* refers to:

   a. the investors or backers.

   b. the actors.

   c. the director.

   d. the producer.

   e. none of the above.

3. In recent years theatrical production on Broadway:

    a. is more open to experimentation.

    b. has become big business.

    c. has been gradually moving away from producing musicals.

    d. has relied largely on grants.

    e. none of the above.

4. A producer can be:

    a. a group of people.

    b. a school.

    c. a department in a college or university.

    d. an individual.

    e. all of the above.

Fill in the Blank

1. The commercial theatre in the United States is centered in _____.

2. In New York, Broadway theatre appeals to the masses, but _____ often has a more limited appeal.

3. The most important consideration for educational theatre is to plan a season that is _____.

4. Community theatre's major concern is selecting plays that _____.

5. LORT is an acronym for _____ that serves as a management association that negotiates contracts with professional theatre unions.

Short Essay   *Use additional paper if necessary.*

1. What is the role of the producer in Broadway productions?

2. What is the importance of nonprofit theatres?

3. What are the duties of a house manager?

4. What are the major differences between Broadway and Off-Broadway theatre?

5. Discuss the major differences between producing shows in amateur theatre and in professional theatre.

Chapter 10
THE AUDIENCE AND THE CRITIC

The primary goal of the chapter is two-fold: to explain the audience-theatre artist relationship and to teach students standards of criticism they can apply to their own viewing of theatrical productions.

Key Concepts

- Since audiences and performers affect each other's reactions, a theatrical production differs from night to night.

- The direct flow of feeling between audience and artist sets theatre and other live arts apart from film and television.

- The audience affects not only the performers but also itself.

- A bonding occurs among audience members at a theatrical production. The bond is difficult to achieve if the audience is sparse or seated apart from one another.

- Different types of plays draw differing audiences.

- The audience has half a contract to fulfill when attending the theatre. They are responsible for becoming acquainted with theatre in order to understand it as an art form.

- Audiences attend the theatre for a number of reasons: to be entertained; to learn of recent, present and imminent change; to confront social issues; to learn about people; to learn from the past; as a reaffirmation of the audience's beliefs; to feel or to experience emotion.

- The average theatergoer is white, middle-aged or older, has a college education, a white-collar job, and a better than average income.

- Other types of people more likely will attend college/university or experimental theatre.

- During recent years, overall and minority attendance at theatrical productions has increased.

- Each audience member is a critic in that he or she has opinions about the production. The major difference between the average theatergoer and the professional reviewer or critic is that the professionals generally better articulate the reasons for a production's success or failure.

- Before evaluating a production, you should examine your own background, feelings, emotions, and beliefs.

- The fundamental difference between a reviewer and a critic is that the former usually writes to a strict deadline while the critic has more leisure for reflection and most often the latter's review is more inclusive of such things as a playwright's entire body of work.

- A review fulfills a number of purposes. It acquaints potential audiences with the production; it allows those who have seen a show to compare their opinions with the reviewer's; it helps audience members relive the experience of attending the production; it helps publicize the production and/or the theatre; it provides instruction; it sometimes influences theatre artists to improve their work; it entertains.

- The critic/reviewer needs a standard on which to base his or her work. One way is to apply Goethe's three questions to a production.

- A review both informs and judges, but must be consistent in its judgment.

- A reviewer or critic needs to find the answers to certain questions before attending a production. These relate to the play's genre and time period, to the theatre company or organization, to the theatre structure, and to the sort of audience the theatre usually draws.

- The reviewer needs to consider if a production's overall style is appropriate and consistent.

- Reviewers need to consider specific questions related to the acting, the directing, and to the various areas of design. They need to judge whether all the artistic elements are subjugated to the whole of the production.

- Less important, except in premiere productions of an original play, the reviewer considers how well the playwright accomplished his purpose.

Additional Information

According to the May 31, 1998, edition of the *New York Times*, Broadway touring shows grossed nearly $800-million in the preceding season. In contrast, they grossed only about $200-million in the mid-1980s. This can be attributed in large part to the attraction of audiences to major musicals such as *Beauty and the Beast* and *Phantom of the Opera*. Obviously, audiences attending these shows are looking for escapism, entertainment, and spectacle.

Further Reading

- *The Little Foxes*
- Any other plays mentioned in the chapter

Group Discussion Topics

- Would you rather see a live play or a television show? Why?
- Why do you suppose a theatre audience is more likely to experience a release of emotions than is a single viewer watching a play or a television show?
- Audiences attend the theatre for a variety of reasons. What do you think would be your most compelling reasons for attending a theatrical production?
- What do you think can be done to attract more college students to the theatre?
- Would you enjoy being a theatre critic? Explain.

Activities

- Attend a play. Ask as many of the audience members as you can why they witnessed the production. Report your findings to the class.
- Attend a play and write a review.
- Read a review in a local newspaper and report to the class on how well you think the reviewer did his or her job.
- Read one of the plays mentioned in the chapter and write a review *only* of the script and how well you think the playwright accomplished his or her purpose.

Chapter 10 Exam Questions

True or False   *Circle the correct answer.*

1. More minorities have been attending the theatre in recent years.
   True   False

2. A theatrical production rarely varies from night to night.
   True   False

3. An audience usually affects itself but not the performers.
   True   False

4. Most people attend the theatre to experience deep emotion.
   True   False

5. Younger people are more likely to attend the theatre than those in their fifties.
   True   False

Multiple Choice   *Circle the correct answer.*

1. Theatres are seeking potential audiences primarily among:
   a. the elderly.
   b. high-school dropouts.
   c. business persons.
   d. students.
   e. single parents.

2. One of the primary purposes of a review is to:
   a. acquaint a potential audience with the production.
   b. publicize a production.
   c. influence theatre artists to change what they're doing.
   d. help audience members to relive the experience of the play.
   e. all of the above.

3. One of the three questions Goethe felt should be used to judge a production is:
   - a. how appropriate was the costuming?
   - b. were the actors professional or amateur?
   - c. was the theatre appropriate for the production?
   - d. was the play worth doing?
   - e. none of the above.

4. Before attending a show, a reviewer should try to learn:
   - a. what other reviewers or critics are likely to attend.
   - b. the play's genre.
   - c. the biographies of the performers.
   - d. if the designers previously have worked together.
   - e. if a director or a dramaturg cast the show.

5. Which of the following is important in judging an actor?
   - a. the person's training.
   - b. past experience in area theatres.
   - c. the performer's sense of timing.
   - d. the person's ties to the area.
   - e. all of the above.

Fill in the Blank

1. A _____ must write or evaluate a production quickly to meet a near deadline.

2. _____ makes a play relevant or important to the time in which it is written.

3. Different types of plays draw different _____.

4. The most common reason for attending a play is _____.

Short Essay   *Use additional paper if necessary.*
1. Discuss two or three of the major purposes of a review.

2. Discuss two of the reasons audiences attend the theatre.

3. What are the major reasons a theatrical production differs from night to night?

4. In what way is each audience member also a critic?

5. What are the differences between a theatre critic and a play reviewer?

Part III
THEATRE HISTORY

Chapter 11
THEATRE'S BEGINNINGS

The primary goal of this chapter is to present information about how theatre began and how it developed in ancient times and in Greece and Rome.

Key Concepts

- Theatre most likely began with a ritualistic form of worship in many different cultures.

- India developed Sanskrit drama which was based on the concept of two types of emotions, that which is deep and that which is fleeting.

- Japanese drama included Noh theatre and Kabuki, the latter of which is the more popular.

- Greek theatre developed in Athens and was a blending of ritual and imitation that began in the sixth century with dithyrambs, hymns to Dionysus, the god of wine and harvest.

- Throughout all of Greek drama, the chorus continued to serve as the unifying force. It acted as a character or sometimes two characters discussing events with each other, and it sometimes served as narrator and messenger.

- Drama was presented at three festivals, but the only plays that survive were presented at the City Dionysia.

- The festivals had a master of revels called an *archon*, who selected the plays, and a *choregoi* who footed any expenses. Playwrights applied to the *archon* for rights to present their drama.

- At the City Dionysia, each playwright was expected to present a trilogy and a satyr play.

- Greece's golden age of drama was the fifth century BC, when all the most important developments in playwriting and production occurred.

- Aeschylus, the first important playwright relied largely on the chorus and used traditional themes for his writing. Although his plays had a plot, they were mostly choral. Aeschylus is credited with introducing a second actor into the plays for the sake of variety, not for conflict. His best work is considered to be the *Orestian Trilogy*.

- The next major writer of tragedy was Sophocles, who is credited with introducing a third actor. He was more interested in the interplay between characters than in the telling of myths and in human beings as determiners of their own fate.

- The third major writer was Euripides who was concerned largely with the human being as an individual. He dealt with the inner conflict of good versus evil. His most widely produced play is *The Trojan Women*.

- Greek comedy related to current events. The plots were more complicated than those of tragedies and more episodic.

- Old Comedy emphasized idea rather than a cause-to-effect relationship of events. The only extant writer of this form is Aristophanes.

- The most celebrated writer of New Comedy was Menander, who wrote more than one hundred plays. New comedy dealt with middle-class citizens.

- Plays were presented outdoors on a flat place at the base of a hill. At first there were no walls or ceilings. An altar to Dionysus was located in the middle of the site. In the fifth century BC, a skene building was added. Later a second floor was used for the appearance of the gods. Little scenery was used.

- The theatre of Dionysus, the most famous Greek theatre, seated about fourteen thousand spectators. Greek theatre used various types of stage machinery including the *deus ex machina*, a crane to lower the gods, and the *ekkyklema*, a cart or platform believed to have carried bodies of actors portraying dead warriors since the Greeks did not show violence on-stage.

- Greek actors were highly respected and highly trained.

- Every type of character had a specific mask.

- Perhaps the most important contribution to Greek theatre was the writings of Aristotle.

- Romans saw imported Greek plays, and Roman writers imitated Greek plays, particularly those by Menander.

- Drama in Rome was first presented at festivals held four times a year. A magistrate, often using some of his own money and with aid from the state, was in charge.

- At first, Roman theatres were temporary structures made of wood. It wasn't until 55 BC that the first permanent theatre was erected. They were elaborate structures with stone columns, arches, and intricate statues and friezes.

- The most popular Roman playwrights were Plautus and Terence. The former wrote a large number of comedies pointing up the idiosyncrasies of individual characters. Terence's style was literary, but his dialog was written in the style of everyday conversation.
- The only Roman tragedies in existence were written by Seneca and were adaptations of Greek plays. Because they were written to be recited rather than produced, they contained much violence.

Additional Information

One of the oldest forms of Roman comedy, the Atellan farce, was characterized by improvisation and stock characters, including the braggart, the gluttonous fool, and the old miser — the model for Shakespeare's Shylock in *The Merchant of Venice* and Molière's Harpagon in *The Miser*. The plots consisted of ludicrous situations involving such things as drunkenness and trickery.

Further Reading

It is recommended that at the very least students read one of the Greek tragedies and one of the comedies.

- *Agamemnon* by Aeschylus
- *Oedipus Rex* (if not already read) or *Antigone* by Sophocles
- *The Trojan Women* by Euripides
- *Lysistrata* or *The Clouds* by Aristaphanes
- *The Menaechmi* by Plautus

Group Discussion Topics

- Explain the connection between ritual and theatre.
- How did the theatre of Greece differ from the theatre of Rome?
- Compare and contrast the role of actors in Greece and Rome.
- The ancient Greeks did not show violence on-stage. What do you think accounts for the difference between Greek culture and ours, in which so many films of violence are shown?
- Do we still use any of the architectural or stage devices that the ancient Greeks originated? Do we employ any modifications of them? Explain.

Activities

- Build a model of a Greek theatre.
- Conduct further research on the Noh and Kabuki theatres and present a demonstration of some of the stylized movements used by the actors.
- Select and stage a scene from Euripides' play *The Trojan Women*.
- In a small group of ten to twelve actors, rehearse and perform a dialog written for the chorus from *The Trojan Women*. Remember that the chorus moved and spoke as if they were one character.

Chapter 11 Exam Questions

True or False   *Circle the correct answer.*

1. The theatre of ancient Rome was superior to that of Greece.

    True   False

2. Kabuki theatre originated in China about 200 BC.

    True   False

3. Actors were highly respected in ancient Greece.

    True   False

4. Dionysus was the god of fire.

    True   False

5. Plato wrote *The Poetics*.

    True   False

Multiple Choice   *Circle the correct answer.*

1. According to legend, the first Greek actor was named:

    a. Aristotle.

    b. Euripides.

    c. Sophocles.

    d. Thespis.

    e. none of the above.

2. Greek tragedies were presented:

    a. in trilogies.

    b. at night.

    c. by priests and noblemen.

    d. entirely in the winter.

    e. all of the above.

3. Roman drama:

    a. was created from Sanskrit drama.

    b. always dealt with comedic themes.

    c. was an imitation of Greek drama.

    d. was enacted by slaves.

    e. none of the above.

4. Theatre most likely began as:

    a. ritualistic worship.

    b. enactments of battles between warring tribes.

    c. tragedy.

    d. a worship of the god of Sparta.

    e. satyr plays.

Fill in the Blank

1. The writer of New Comedy was _____.

2. Aeschylus's best work is considered to be _____.

3. The type of plays Seneca wrote were intended to be _____ rather than _____.

4. *The Clouds* and *The Frogs* were written by _____.

5. The _____ was a crane to lower the gods to the stage floor.

Short Essay   *Use additional paper if necessary.*

1. What were the major differences between the way plays were presented in ancient Greece and in ancient Rome?

2. Define New Comedy.

3. Discuss the evolutions of ancient Greek drama.

4. Explain the role of the *archon* in producing Greek plays.

5. Discuss the role of the chorus in ancient Greek plays.

Chapter 12
MEDIEVAL THEATRE

The primary goal for this chapter is to provide knowledge about the development of theatre and drama during the Medieval period in Europe.

Key Concepts

- After the fall of the Roman Empire in 476, little in the way of theatre was presented for several hundred years. The Roman Catholic church felt theatre was evil and sacrilegious. Those actors who continued to perform were refused the sacrament of communion.

- Drama was reborn as part of the church service in the form of tropes presented by clergymen at the church's major yearly events. Initially, the tropes were in Latin but later were presented in the local language.

- As the tropes became more elaborate, so did their presentation so that the staging consisted of *sedes* (mansions) for each separate scene and a *platea*, or central acting place. The tropes were becoming more secular.

- By the thirteenth century, presentations were so involved that they were moved to the west side of the church. In the next couple of centuries, secular groups assumed responsibility for their production.

- One of the most popular forms was the *Corpus Christi* play which emphasized transubstantiation. The production grew to encompass all of creation.

- Trade guilds and special societies now produced the plays, but they still needed church approval. Soon the productions moved away from the church.

- In England, plays were presented using ancient amphitheatres and pageant wagons. They often consisted of a great number of episodic scenes using many mansions. The scenes bore no relationship to one another except that they were based in the Christian Bible. There were numerous special effects and a great deal of violence. Beginning in the sixteenth century, the plays contained humor.

- By the end of the fourteenth century the plays were combined into a single presentation or cycle. Humor now often centered on wives.

- Guilds or town councils hired directors who were in charge of the technical aspects of production, as well as the acting.
- The three important forms of drama to evolve from the church presentations were mystery plays, miracle plays, and morality plays. The first dealt with the life of Christ, the second with the lives of saints and martyrs, and the last with Everyman's attempt to save his soul. During the sixteenth century, morality plays became more secularized.
- Secular drama that developed during the Middle Ages included the farce, which was concerned with humanity's depravity, and interludes, comic plays performed by traveling players for wealthy citizens.
- Medieval drama began to decline during the sixteenth century because the social structure was changing; there was an increased interest in classical learning; actors began to travel as professionals, and there was dissension in the church.

Additional Information

- "Minstrels," a generic term used for professional entertainers of the Middle Ages, flourished from the eleventh through the fifteenth centuries. Even though the church looked down on the minstrels, they played a part in early religious festivities and probably influenced the beginnings of liturgical drama.
- The pageant wagon was the stage or cart on which a medieval religious play was performed. It consisted of two rooms, the lower one curtained off as a dressing room, though it could be used to represent hell. Later the name was transferred to the traveling entertainments, not necessarily religious, of which the Lord Mayor's Show in London is a late survivor.

Further Reading

- *The Second Shepherd's Play*
- *Everyman*

Group Discussion Topics

- During the several hundred years following the fall of the Roman Empire and the beginning of liturgical drama, what sort of theatrical entertainment existed and how did it manage to survive?
- Why did the liturgical dramas move outside the church?
- Describe the staging and production of liturgical dramas.
- What were guilds and what role did they play in the development of drama?
- What is meant by characters in morality plays being called allegorical? Give examples.

Activities

- Build a model of a mansion as used in medieval theatre.
- Write your own morality play. Cast the parts and read it aloud in class.
- Research and present a report on the special effects or "secrets" used in Medieval plays.
- Rehearse and present the play *Everyman* in class.
- More fully investigate and write a paper on the cycle plays in England.

Chapter 12 Exam Questions

True or False   *Circle the correct answer.*

1. The church has always advocated having theatre activities.

   True   False

2. The first play of the medieval period was written by a group of minstrels.

   True   False

3. Early liturgical drama was performed only in the church and by priests.

   True   False

4. Mystery plays dealt with the life of Christ.

   True   False

5. Guild actors were mostly amateurs.

   True   False

Multiple Choice   *Circle the correct answer.*

1. The most important forms of drama to evolve from the church presentations were:

   a. comedy, tragedy, and pastoral plays.

   b. farce, mystery plays, and medieval plays.

   c. mystery plays, miracle plays, and morality plays.

   d. interludes.

   e. none of the above.

2. Cycle plays were:

   a. a collection of all plays written throughout the church year.

   b. plays that dealt with the cycle of life, from birth to death.

   c. plays that dealt with the cycle of the moon and harvesting seasons.

   d. plays about shepherds and their flocks.

   e. none of the above.

3. Cycle plays often made fun of:
   a. priests and nuns.
   b. shrewish wives.
   c. stingy husbands.
   d. poorly behaved children.
   e. all of the above.

4. Medieval theatre included:
   a. secular dramas.
   b. violence on-stage.
   c. women as actors.
   d. children as actors.
   e. all of the above.

5. *Abraham and Isaac* was:
   a. a comedy.
   b. a minstrel show.
   c. completely reverential in tone.
   d. secular.
   e. all of the above.

Fill in the Blank

1. Liturgical playlets were also called _____.

2. Allegorical characters appeared in _____.

3. A _____ carried two or more mansions and was designed to move from place to place.

4. Staging or scenery in the medieval church consisted of mansions or _____.

5. The general acting area in churches and cathedrals was called _____.

Short Essay *Use additional paper if necessary.*

1. Discuss the reasons theatrical activity began to decline in Europe during the sixteenth century.

2. Explain the course of events leading up to theatres moving away from the Christian church.

3. Define and discuss the three most important forms of drama to come from the medieval age.

4. What did Augustine mean when he said that "the theatres are falling nearly everywhere"? Give the historical and political context for his statement.

Chapter 13

RENAISSANCE THEATRE

The primary goal for this chapter is to present a brief history of theatre during the Renaissance period (1400–1500).

Key Concepts

- Three events are important in the rebirth of learning during the Renaissance: the fall of Constantinople when fleeing monks carried ancient manuscripts with them out into the lay world; the spread of the printing press, and the rediscovery of Seneca's tragedies.

- There were huge changes in theatre from small bands or actors performing in homes or booths to sophisticated plays and scenery.

- In Italy, writers imitated Plautus, Seneca, and Terence. It was largely due to Seneca's influence that the rigid rules of neoclassicism were formulated. One of the most binding was there had to be a strict adherence to the unities of time, place, and action.

- Niccolò Machiavelli's *La Mandragola*, often considered the masterpiece of Italian Renaissance drama, followed the classic format but was much more original, as well as being cynical in approach.

- The pastoral, popular during the sixteenth century, dealt with rural folk, as well as mythical characters, and plots that involved romantic love.

- A popular form, the *intermezzi*, a series of short scenes or plays presented along with neoclassic tragedy, was replaced in popularity by opera, which by 1650 spread through much of Europe.

- Italy contributed most to theatre through staging. Sebastiano Serlio wrote a book showing how a theatre should be constructed in existing buildings. He described three settings — tragic, comic, and pastoral — all of which used false perspective and were to be used for all plays.

- Later, permanent theatres were erected. The oldest is the Teatro Olimpico, designed by Andrea Palladio. After Palladio's death, his pupil Vincenzo Scamozzi added his own ideas. He followed the Roman plan but added false perspective in the raked floor and three-dimensional background.

- The Teatro Farnese was the first theatre to use a proscenium arch.

- Various methods were developed to change scenery. One was Serlion wings or modified Greek periaktoi. Another was V-shaped wings that stood one behind the other and were developed by Nicola Sabbattini.

- The *commedia dell'arte*, popular for a century, involved stock characters and improvisation. Actors were assigned certain characters which they continued to play all their lives.

- Although Spain was influenced to a degree by neoclassicism, its drama developed somewhat differently and had a more lasting literary value than that in the rest of Europe.

- The most popular Spanish drama was the *auto sacramental*, which was similar to the medieval mystery and miracle plays in subject matter but akin to the morality play in the use of allegorical characters.

- Spain's most prolific playwright was Lope de Vega, believed to have written more than 1800 plays.

- In Spain, plays were presented either in court theatres or *corrales*, or open courtyards.

- In Elizabethan England, actors at first were defined by law as vagabonds and rogues. In 1572, a new law stated they either could be licensed or could perform under the patronage of a nobleman. Still, it took time before the general public accepted them.

- Elizabethan theatre had its basis in several sources: schools, Inns of Court, and professional acting companies.

- The three greatest Elizabethan dramatists were Ben Jonson, Christopher Marlowe, and William Shakespeare. Jonson used satire to denounce middle-class vices and foolish actions. Marlowe wrote few plays, but helped free Elizabethan drama from the restriction of medieval forms. Shakespeare wrote in various genres, but his tragedies are considered his greatest work.

- There were two types of theatre in Elizabethan England: private and public. The former was more exclusive. The popular theatres, such as Shakespeare's Globe, were located outside of town.

- Acting companies at the public theatres consisted of ten to twenty men and three to five boy apprentices. The boys played the female roles.

Additional Information

- Torquato Tasso's *L'Aminta* (1573) is generally considered the first pastoral play. The form is identified by the depiction of a happy outcome of faithful love in a remote, rural setting. One of the best known is Giambattista Guarini's *The Faithful Shepherd* (1590), which influenced the later development of romantic literature in France and England. It is filled with idealistic language and lofty ideas.

- By the mid-sixteenth century in Spain, *autos sacramentales*, allegorical plays depicting eucharistic themes, were performed at the feast of *Corpus Christi*. The form culminated with Pedro Calderón, sole author of Madrid's *autos* from 1648 to 1681. In 1765 these works were suppressed under the Bourbon Enlightenment.

- The Lord Chamberlain's Men was the finest of the Elizabethan theatre companies. It was founded in 1594 under the patronage of the Lord Chamberlain, Lord Hunsdon. The original company comprised Cuthbert and Richard Burbage, Thomas Pope, Augustine Phillips, John Heminges, William Kempe, and William Shakespeare.

- Serlio's comic and tragic settings were street scenes, while the pastoral setting was a wooded area.

Further Reading

Recommended:

- *The Tragical History of Dr. Faustus*
- Either *Hamlet* or *Othello*

Supplementary:

- Any of Ben Jonson's plays
- Any other plays mentioned in the chapter

Group Discussion Topics

- What three events brought about the renaissance of learning?
- What were the neoclassic unities and from what were they adapted?
- The Italian Renaissance is known for the contributions of its scenic designers. Discuss the conventions they brought into use that have greatly impacted our current practices.
- Why do you suppose *commedia dell'arte* performances became popular?
- What were Shakespeare's most important contributions to the theatre?

Activities

- Draw costume designs for two or three of the stock characters in the *commedia dell'arte*.

- Build a model of an Elizabethan theatre.

- Write a one-act neoclassical play. Be sure to follow the unities of time, place, and action. Now present the play in class.

- Rehearse and perform a scene from *Hamlet*.

- Do further research on the work of the Italian scenic designers and present the information to your class. Include visual examples of their work.

Chapter 13 Exam Questions

True or False   *Circle the correct answer.*

1. Italian playwrights contributed greatly to the field of dramatic literature.
     True   False

2. Neoclassical plays were loosely formatted.
     True   False

3. *La Mandragola* dealt with comic stock characters.
     True   False

4. The *intermezzi* originally was a series of unrelated scenes that contained singing and dancing.
     True   False

5. Stage floors were raked to help give the illusion of distance.
     True   False

Multiple Choice   *Circle the correct answer.*

1. Shakespeare is credited with:
     a. comedies and histories.
     b. tragedies.
     c. having written thirty-eight plays.
     d. being England's greatest playwright.
     e. all of the above.

2. The word *renaissance* means:
     a. bringing back popular works.
     b. breaking away.
     c. reawakening.
     d. using unities.
     e. none of the above.

3. It is believed that the public theatres of Elizabethan England:

    a. used no scenery.

    b. had three levels where action could take place.

    c. had an unroofed open pit where the groundlings would stand.

    d. did not have artificial lighting.

    e. all of the above.

4. In his book, *Architettura*, Serlio:

    a. advocated painting the stage floor in squares that became smaller and smaller toward the back.

    b. described how to construct theatres in existing buildings.

    c. recommended the use of false perspective.

    d. all of the above.

5. The first theatre to use a framing device was:

    a. the Theatre of Dionysus.

    b. *corrales* in Spain.

    c. the Teatro Farnese.

    d. the Globe Theatre.

    e. the *commedia dell'arte* stage.

Fill in the Blank

1. *The Tragical History of Dr. Faustus* was written by _____.

2. Serlio described three _____ that could be used for all plays.

3. *The Spanish Tragedy* by Thomas Kyd set the example for

    _____.

4. Spain's best-known and most prolific playwright was

    _____.

5. Comic visual business in *commedia dell'arte* was called

    _____.

Short Essay   *Use additional paper if necessary.*

1. Discuss what political, social, and economic events brought on the Renaissance.

2. Discuss Italy's greatest contributions to the theatre during the Renaissance.

3. Discuss the development of Spanish drama during the Renaissance.

4. Comment on the early origins of English theatre during the Renaissance.

5. Explain the social standing of actors before and during the reign of Elizabeth I.

Chapter 14

SEVENTEENTH- AND EIGHTEENTH-CENTURY THEATRE

The primary goal for this chapter is to explain the evolution of theatre and drama throughout Europe during the seventeenth and eighteenth centuries.

Key Concepts

- During the Restoration, new English theatres had proscenium arches and an apron projecting into the audience.

- The most significant dramatic genre was comedy of manners, which satirized the social customs of the time. The most notable playwright was William Congreve whose best play was *The Way of the World*.

- Most popular during the reign of Queen Anne was sentimental comedy, which was characterized by false emotions and sentimentality over the misfortunes of others. A related form was bourgeois tragedy. The only difference was that the former ended happily and the latter unhappily.

- Also popular were pantomime and ballad opera.

- Oliver Goldsmith wrote *She Stoops to Conquer*, which was an attempt to return to comedy that was funny.

- David Garrick introduced a natural style of acting and insisted on closely supervising rehearsals. He used three-dimensional scenery, concealed stage lighting from the audience, and insisted that spectators no longer sit on-stage.

- As part of an effort to raise awareness of the arts, Cardinal Richelieu had a theatre built in the Palais Cardinal. He also established the French Academy. Playwrights adhered strictly to neoclassicism and believed that an important element of drama should be verisimilitude.

- Pierre Corneille and Jean Racine were the most important writers of the Academy. Corneille's most successful play was *Le Cid*, a tragicomedy, which became one of the most popular plays of the century. Racine was the greatest writer of French classical tragedy.

- The most important French playwright was Molière, who introduced literary comedy into France. His masterpiece, however, is *The Misanthrope*, which is closer to comedy of manners.

- Caroline Neuber, an actress who headed her own troupe, raised the level of acting and drama in Germany by insisting on careful rehearsals, high personal morals, and the presentation of plays with high literary standards.

Additional Information

- A masque was a spectacular form of entertainment that combined music and poetry with scenery and elaborate costumes. The form, which reached its peak at the English court between 1600 and 1640, was originally derived from a primitive folk ritual featuring the arrival of guests, usually in disguise, bringing gifts to a king or nobleman. With his household, the nobleman then joined the visitors in a ceremonial dance, which was followed by flattering speeches in the host's honor.

- Cardinal Richelieu (Armand-Jean du Plessis, 1585–1642), was a statesman who, as chief of the royal council under King Louis XIII, was for many years the virtual ruler of France. He helped establish a permanent professional theatre in Paris and raised the status of actors. He wrote a number of plays with a committee of playwrights including Corneille, with whom he later argued about his share of the plot.

- One of Moliére's often-produced comedies is *Tartuffe*, the tale of a rogue who has wormed his way into the admirations and affections of a gullible merchant named Orgon. Considered by many to be Molière's masterpiece, however, is *The Misanthrope*, a different sort of writing that comes closer to comedy of manners. The central character is Alceste, who has become so bitter about society's superficiality and hypocrisy that he wants to withdraw from the world. A succession of scenes reveal his justification in criticizing gossips, fops, and pretentious poets. At the same time, the play reveals his own intolerance, his refusal to compromise, and his obsessions with humankind's faults.

- The King's Men, at first called the Lord Chamberlain's Men, was the company for which Shakespeare created most of his works. It was founded in 1594 and occupied the Theatre, built by James Burbage. In 1599 the company moved to the Globe. In 1603, after the death of Elizabeth I, the company came under the patronage of James I and became known as the King's Men.

- Inigo Jones (1573–1652) was an English architect and artist. He was the first to be associated with scene design in England. He studied in Italy and worked in Denmark until 1604, when he was called upon by Prince Henry not only to work as court architect but also to design the masques for court. Jones introduced many scenic devices, including the use of the proscenium arch, revolving screens, back cloths, and flats painted and arranged in perspective.

Further Reading

- *The Way of the World*
- *The Miser* or *Tartuffe*

Group Discussion Topics

- What social and political activities influenced changes in seventeenth- and eighteenth-century theatre?
- Which countries contributed most to theatre during the seventeenth and eighteenth centuries?
- Why do you suppose sentimental comedy and bourgeois tragedy became so popular during the reign of Queen Anne?
- Why do you suppose Molière often is called the French Shakespeare? Is this justified? Why?

Activities

- Investigate the trend toward romanticism during the eighteenth century in Germany and report your findings to the class.
- Using the staging ideas brought to England by Inigo Jones, build and display a model of a theatre that may have been used in England during the eighteenth century.
- Do additional research and then present an oral or written report to the class on the role of women as actor-managers during the eighteenth century.
- Create costume designs for a masque as it may have been produced during the seventeenth century.
- Present a speech from one of Shakespeare's plays in the more declamatory style actors may have used during the eighteenth century.

Chapter 14 Exam Questions

True or False   *Circle the correct answer.*

1. By the eighteenth century, Italy no longer dominated the technical aspects of European theatre.

   True   False

2. Racine was the greatest writer of German comedies.

   True   False

3. The Restoration period began when Charles II was restored to the throne.

   True   False

4. Molière is credited with introducing sentimental comedy into France.

   True   False

Multiple Choice   *Circle the correct answer.*

1. The invention of the steam engine meant that:

   a. commerce would increase.

   b. people could afford to attend theatre.

   c. cities could support the growth of theatres.

   d. all of the above.

2. Comedy of manners is also called:

   a. bourgeois comedy.

   b. pantomime.

   c. Restoration comedy.

   d. ballad opera.

   e. none of the above.

3. Oliver Goldsmith wrote:

    a. funny comedies.

    b. bourgeois tragedy.

    c. plays based on Roman models.

    d. *commedia dell'arte* sketches.

    e. sweeping epics.

4. The French Academy was concerned with:

    a. the rules of neoclassicism.

    b. tragicomedy.

    c. acting companies.

    d. comedy of manners.

    e. all of the above.

Fill in the Blank

1. "Verisimilitude" means the appearance of _____
   on the stage.

2. Jean-Baptiste Poquelin is better known as _____.

3. Shakespeare worked with the theatre company known as
   _____.

4. George Lilo's *The London Merchant* is an example of
   _____ tragedy.

Short Essay   *Use additional paper if necessary.*

1. Who was David Garrick and what did he bring to the theatre?

2. Define comedy of manners and name a playwright famous for the form.

3. Who was Corneille? What transpired in his relationship to the French Academy?

Chapter 15

NINETEENTH- TO TWENTY-FIRST-CENTURY THEATRE

The primary goal of this chapter is to acquaint students with changes that took place in theatre and drama during the nineteenth, twentieth, and early twenty-first centuries.

Key Concepts

- Throughout the past two hundred years, there have been more changes in form and style than ever before.
- Romanticism taught that a person has only to follow his or her instincts to know what is right.
- Melodrama inspired the development of common heroes such as the American Indian, Davy Crockett, and Jack Tar. The most widely-produced nineteenth-century play was *Uncle Tom's Cabin*.
- Theatre continued to increase in popularity during the nineteenth century.
- Until the 1830s, the most popular type of acting troupe was the repertory company. This was followed by the star system and then the combination company.
- The Theatrical Syndicate demanded that local theatre owners work with it exclusively in booking shows.
- Realism developed as a result of oppressive political and economic conditions.
- A significant change in staging was the use of gas lights and, by the 1880s, the use of electricity. By the end of the century, the box set also was in use.
- Henrik Ibsen, the father of modern drama, dealt with socially significant themes and did more than any other playwright of the time to establish realism as an integral part of drama.
- After realism came naturalism with the belief that a playwright's only job was to observe and record events.
- The most important playwright of the late nineteenth and early twentieth centuries was George Bernard Shaw. Other important playwrights were Oscar Wilde and John Millington Synge.

- In Russia, Anton Chekhov wrote plays based on contemporary Russian life that presented characters defeated by circumstances.
- George II, Duke of Saxe-Meiningen, generally is credited with being the first director.
- Since plays were subject to censorship in much of Europe, a number of independent theatres were established.
- The eclectic approach to theatre received impetus through the work of director Max Reinhardt, who believed each play required a different style of presentation.
- Adolphe Appia and Edward Gordon Craig sought to create an environment that was fitting for each play.
- One of the best-known expressionist playwrights was August Strindberg of Sweden.
- Expressionism was advanced in America largely through the work of Eugene O'Neill.
- Developing at the same time as expressionism was surrealism, which involves breaking down barriers between the conscious and subconscious worlds.
- Epic theatre, or theatre of alienation, was established by Berthold Brecht who developed a theory of distancing to point up social problems rather than having audiences identify strongly with characters.
- The forerunners of absurdism were Jean-Paul Sartre and Albert Camus, while Eugéne Ionesco began writing absurdist drama. However, Samuel Beckett's *Waiting for Godot* is considered the archetypal absurdist drama.
- Eugene O'Neill became America's first important playwright. Arthur Miller and Tennessee Williams, the two most important postwar playwrights, wrote psychological realism. Coming to prominence a decade later was Edward Albee.
- The world's most commercially successful writer of comedy is Neil Simon.
- Theatre in the United States began to come into its own in the early part of the twentieth century.
- Important influences on American theatre were Artaud's Theatre of Cruelty, Jerzy Grotowski's Polish Laboratory Theatre, and the Living Theatre of Julian Beck and Judith Malina and later Joseph Chaikin's The Open Theatre.
- Happenings, which were unrehearsed, involved a multimedia performance.
- Important in recent and contemporary theatre is performance art which takes a multimedia approach.

- Postmodernism redefines art in new and unexpected ways in drawing on a number of sources for any particular production.
- The terrorist attacks of September 11, 2001, influenced and affected theatre financially as well as artistically.
- Current Broadway theatre stages many revivals and stays with the tried and true.

Additional Information

- The Theatrical Syndicate monopoly was formed in 1896, and by 1903 it governed all the top theatrical productions in America. Partners Charles Frohman, Marc Klaw, and Abraham Erlanger joined with Alfred Hayman, who leased the most important theatres in the west, and Fred Nixon and Fred Zimmerman, who controlled Philadelphia and the rest of the mid-Atlantic region, to form the Syndicate.
- Émile Zola (1840–1902) was a French novelist and dramatist who had an important influence on European drama. He disliked the facile, optimistic works of such dramatists as Scribe and thought a play should be a "slice of life" thrown on the stage without embellishment or artifice. He set out his theories in a number of articles, later published in two volumes, *Le Naturalisme au Théâtre* (1878) and *Nos Auteurs Dramatiques* (1881). He demonstrated his theories in his play *Thérèse Raquin*.

Further Reading

- *An Enemy of the People* or *A Doll's House*
- *Uncle Vanya* or *The Cherry Orchard*
- *Mother Courage and Her Children*
- *Long Day's Journey Into Night* or *The Hairy Ape*
- *The Glass Menagerie* or *A Streetcar Named Desire*
- *Three Tall Women* or *Who's Afraid of Virginia Woolf?*
- *Brighton Beach Memoirs*
- Any other plays or playwrights mentioned in the chapter

Group Discussion Topics

- Which of the many "isms" that developed during the nineteenth and twentieth century are the most important to contemporary theatre? Why?
- What conditions brought about the rise of the director?
- What is the purpose of slice-of-life drama?
- Why do you suppose George Bernard Shaw is considered to be such an important playwright?
- How do you think the terrorist attacks of September 11, 2001, affected professional theatre in the U.S.?

Activities

- Create and stage a happening.
- Develop a performance art piece and perform it for your class.
- Stage a scene from an expressionist play.
- Do additional research about contemporary performance artists and share the information in class.
- Many of Ibsen's plays often were thought to be scandalous. Investigate why this is so.
- Do additional research on Bertolt Brecht's theatre of alienation and share your information with the class.

Chapter 15 Exam Questions

True or False   *Circle the correct answer.*

1. Much of melodrama's popularity was due to spectacle.

   True   False

2. Theatre of the absurd is an example of naturalism.

   True   False

3. August Strindberg wrote surrealist plays.

   True   False

4. The Industrial Revolution placed theatre within the reach of the common people.

   True   False

5. The most important playwright of the late nineteenth and early twentieth century in England was George Bernard Shaw.

   True   False

6. Absurdist theatre deals primarily with the tragic heroes.

   True   False

Multiple Choice   *Circle the correct answer.*

1. Melodrama brought us:

   a. realistic plots.

   b. common heroes.

   c. a slice of life.

   d. the work of Maurice Maeterlinck.

   e. none of the above.

2. Melodrama traditionally promotes:

   a. a realistic view of the world.

   b. a view of women's rights not seen before.

   c. stereotypes.

   d. theatre of cruelty.

   e. all of the above.

3. The following play is an example of absurdism:
   a. *Mother Courage and Her Children.*
   b. *Show Boat.*
   c. *The Lady of the Camellias.*
   d. *Uncle Tom's Cabin.*
   e. *Waiting for Godot.*

4. Joseph Chaikin was the founder of:
   a. the Open Theatre.
   b. the Polish Laboratory Theatre.
   c. the American Theatre.
   d. *The Lower Depths.*
   e. none of the above.

Fill in the Blank

1. Davy Crockett and Jack Tar are examples of _____.

2. Another name for epic theatre is _____.

3. The Duke of Saxe-Meiningen generally is considered to be the first theatrical _____.

4. Gilbert and Sullivan wrote _____ satirizing the upper class.

5. Max Reinhardt believed that each play required a different _____ of presentation.

Short Essay   *Use additional paper if necessary.*
1. Who was Henrik Isben and what was his contribution to theatre?

2. When did historical accuracy in costumes and sets become the norm?

3. Name and discuss two or three of the early influences on the development of American theatre.

4. Define postmodernism in relation to theatre.

ANSWER KEY

Answer Key

Following are the answers for the objective chapter exam questions. The essay parts of the chapter exams are based on a reading of the text and should be evaluated at the instructor's discretion.

Chapter 1

True or False

1. false
2. true
3. false
4. true

Multiple Choice

1. a
2. d
3. d
4. c
5. d

Fill in the Blank

1. life
2. otherness
3. temporal
4. framework
5. flats

Short Essay

1. see page 11: "The Mimetic Instinct"
2. answers will vary
3. see pages 24-25: "The Elements of Drama"
4. see page 26: "Theatre Conventions"
5. see page 22

Chapter 2

True or False

1. false
2. true
3. true
4. false
5. false

Multiple Choice

1. b
2. a
3. b
4. e

Fill in the Blank

1. French scene
2. story play
3. climax
4. Episodic structure
5. denouement or falling action

Short Essay

1. see page 32: "The Story Play"
2. see page 33: "Frame of Reference"
3. see page 36: "Conflict and Opposition"
4. see pages 36-38: "Elements of Plot"
5. see pages 47-50: "Other Types of Structure"

Chapter 3

True or False

1. false
2. false
3. true
4. true
5. true

Multiple Choice

1. a
2. c
3. d
4. c
5. a

Fill in the Blank

1. Farce
2. wins
3. stock characters
4. presentational and representational

Short Essay

1. see page 64: "Types of Comedy"
2. see pages 58-59: "Tragedy"
3. see page 59

Chapter 4

True or False

1. false
2. true
3. false
4. true
5. true

Multiple Choice

1. e
2. e
3. d
4. c

Fill in the Blank

1. furthest
2. thrust stage
3. flats
4. proscenium
5. fly space

Short Essay

1. see pages 74-86: "The Proscenium Theatre," "The Arena Theatre," "The Thrust Stage," and "Environmental Theatre"
2. see page 76
3. see page 76
4. see page 87: "Off-stage Areas"

Chapter 5

True or False

1. false
2. false
3. true

Multiple Choice

1. e
2. a
3. d
4. a
5. e

Fill in the Blank

1. characters
2. flashback
3. revelation

Short Essay

1. see page 106: "Dialog"
2. see page 110: "Planning the Exposition"
3. see pages 104-106: "Characterization"
4. see pages 104-106: "Characterization"
5. see pages 99-102

Chapter 6

True or False

1. true
2. false
3. true
4. true
5. false
6. true

Multiple Choice

1. a
2. e
3. d
4. a
5. c

Fill in the Blank

1. call attention
2. actor
3. Grotowski
4. improvise
5. union

Short Essay

1. see pages 125-126: "The Internal Approach"
2. see pages 127-128: "The External Approach"
3. see pages 125-128: "The Internal Approach" and "The External Approach"
4. see pages 128-134: "Developing a Character"

Chapter 7

True or False

1. false
2. true
3. true
4. false

Multiple Choice

1. d
2. b
3. e
4. e

Fill in the Blank

1. blocking
2. closed
3. dress rehearsal
4. emotional
5. movement

Short Essay

1. see pages 148-150: "Anticipating Design and Blocking"
2. see pages 150-152: "Casting the Play"
3. see pages 140-141: "Analyzing the Script"
4. see page 141: "Finding an Overall Concept"
5. see pages 152-159: "Rehearsing the Play"

Chapter 8

True or False

1. true
2. false
3. true
4. true
5. false

Multiple Choice

1. e
2. d
3. b
4. a
5. e

Fill in the Blank

1. character
2. hand prop
3. symmetrical
4. set dressing

Short Essay

1. see pages 172-173: "Balance and Harmony"
2. see pages 173-175: "Planning a Setting"
3. see pages 196-202: "A Multimedia Approach" and "Computer-Aided Design"
4. see page 187

Chapter 9

True or False

1. false
2. false
3. true
4. false
5. true

Multiple Choice

1. b
2. a
3. b
4. e

Fill in the Blank

1. New York
2. Off-Broadway
3. balanced
4. draw well
5. League of Resident Theatres

Short Essay

1. see pages 208-217: "Broadway and Off-Broadway Theatre"
2. see pages 206-208: "Nonprofit Theatre"
3. see page 217: "Members of the Business Staff"
4. see page 210
5. see pages 205-218

Chapter 10

True or False

1. true
2. false
3. false
4. false
5. false

Multiple Choice

1. d
2. e
3. d
4. b
5. c

Fill in the Blank

1. reviewer
2. Immediacy or Universality
3. audiences
4. to be entertained

Short Essay

1. see page 235: "Purposes of a Review"
2. see pages 223-226: "Why Audiences Attend Theatre"
3. see pages 220-223
4. see page 231: "The Audience Member as Critic"
5. see page 234: "Critic Versus Reviewer"

Chapter 11

True or False

1. false
2. false
3. true
4. false
5. false

Multiple Choice

1. d
2. a
3. c
4. a

Fill in the Blank

1. Menander
2. the Oresteian Trilogy
3. recited; produced
4. Aristophanes
5. deus ex machina

Short Essay

1. see pages 256-257: "Roman Theatre"
2. see pages 254-255
3. see pages 247-248: "The Development of Drama"
4. see pages 248-249: "Theatre Festivals and Theatrical Productions"
5. see pages 247-248: "The Development of Drama"

Chapter 12

True or False

1. false
2. false
3. true
4. true
5. true

Multiple Choice

1. c
2. a
3. b
4. e
5. c

Fill in the Blank

1. tropes
2. morality plays
3. pageant wagon
4. *sedes*
5. *platea*

Short Essay

1. see page 271: "Secular Drama"
2. see page 264: "Moving Outside the Church"
3. see pages 270-271
4. see page 261

Chapter 13

True or False

1. false
2. false
3. false
4. true
5. true

Multiple Choice

1. e
2. c
3. e
4. d
5. c

Fill in the Blank

1. Christopher Marlowe
2. settings (or sets)
3. Revenge Tragedy
4. Lope de Vega
5. *lazzi*

Short Essay

1. see pages 273-274: "A Time of Great Change"
2. see pages 274-278: "The Italian Renaissance"
3. see page 279: "Spanish Theatre"
4. see pages 280-281: "Origins"
5. see pages 280-288: "The Theatre of Elizabethan England"

Chapter 14

True or False

1. false
2. false
3. true
4. false

Multiple Choice

1. d
2. c
3. a
4. a

Fill in the Blank

1. truth
2. Moliére
3. the King's Men
4. bourgeois

Short Essay

1. see page 294
2. see pages 291-292: "The Restoration"
3. see page 295: "Cardinal Richelieu and the French Academy"

Chapter 15

True or False

1. true
2. false
3. false
4. true
5. true
6. false

Multiple Choice

1. b
2. c
3. e
4. a

Fill in the Blank

1. common heroes
2. theatre of alienation
3. director
4. operettas
5. style

Short Essay

1. see pages 307-308: "The Well-Made Play"
2. see page 306: "Advances in Staging"
3. see pages 326-328: "Influences on American Theatre"
4. see pages 328-329: "Postmodernism"

About the Author

Marsh Cassady is the author of more than fifty books including novels, true crime, biography, collections of plays, short stories and haiku, and books on theatre and storytelling. His plays have been widely performed in the United States (including Off-Broadway) and in Mexico.

A former actor/director and university professor, he has a Ph.D. in theatre, is a member of Actors' Equity Association and the Dramatists Guild, and has worked with more than a hundred productions. In addition, Cassady has taught various creative writing courses at UCSD and elsewhere. A former small press publisher, he also has been editor of three magazines. Since the early 1980s he has conducted all-genre writing workshops in San Diego and in Playas de Rosarito, Baja California Norte, Mexico, where he has lived since 1997. While teaching at Montclair State in the 70s, he started a playwriting program that included classes, workshops, and individual projects. He has won regional and national awards in the U.S. in playwriting, fiction, nonfiction, and haiku.

Cassady writes editorials, a column and occasional articles for *The Baja Times*, and his digital art and ceramic sculptures are exhibited in several galleries. He continues to write books in various genres.

Order Form

Meriwether Publishing, Ltd.
PO Box 7710
Colorado Springs, CO 80933-7710
Phone: 800-937-5297   Fax: 719-594-9916
Website: www.meriwether.com

Please send me the following books:

_____	**An Introduction to: The Art of Theatre #BK-B288** by Marsh Cassady *A comprehensive text — past, present, and future*	**$24.95**
_____	**An Introduction to: The Art of Theatre Teacher's Guide #BK-B290** by Marsh Cassady	**$19.95**
_____	**Everything About Theatre! #BK-B200** by Robert L. Lee *The guidebook of theatre fundamentals*	**$19.95**
_____	**Let's Put on a Show! #BK-B231** by Adrea Gibbs *A beginner's theatre handbook for young actors*	**$19.95**
_____	**Funny Business #BK-B212** by Marsh Cassady *An introduction to comedy*	**$19.95**
_____	**Acting Games #BK-B168** by Marsh Cassady *A textbook of theatre games and improvisations*	**$17.95**
_____	**The Theatre and You #BK-B115** by Marsh Cassady *An introductory text on all aspects of theatre*	**$15.95**

These and other fine Meriwether Publishing books are available at your local bookstore or direct from the publisher. Use the handy order form on this page. Check our website or call for current prices.

Name:_____ e-mail:_____

Organization name: _____

Address: _____

City: _____ State:_____

Zip: _____ Phone: _____

❑ **Check enclosed**
❑ **Visa / MasterCard / Discover #** _____

Signature: _____   *Expiration date:* _____ / _____
(required for credit card orders)

Colorado residents: Please add 3% sales tax.
Shipping: Include $3.95 for the first book and 75¢ for each additional book ordered.

❑ *Please send me a copy of your complete catalog of books and plays.*